A Young Person's Guide to

Show Jumping

To succeed in show jumping it is vital to learn the right techniques from the outset. Note this young Pony Club rider's good hands, maintaining contact with her pony, the balance in her upper body and her solid lower leg position. Her head is up and she is looking where she is going. The result is a very relaxed and happy pony.

A Young Person's Guide to
Show Jumping

TIM STOCKDALE

with Judith Draper

A PONY CLUB PUBLICATION

First Published 2004
© 2004 The Pony Club

Line drawings: Maggie Raynor
Photography: Martha and Iian Shaw, Equestrian Services Thorney
Design and typesetting: Alan Hamp
© Frontispiece: Pleasure Prints, Walton-on-Thames, Surrey
Produced for The Pony Club by Barbara Cooper

A catalogue record of this book is available
from the British Library

ISBN 0-9541531-9-7

The Pony Club
Stoneleigh Park
Kenilworth
Warwickshire CV8 2RW

Printed and bound in England by HALSTAN, Amersham

Contents

Preface

This book is for young riders who are keen to improve their show jumping performance. I hope it will help them to identify any riding problems which they may be having and to quickly sort them out.

Sharing experience is so important and I have tried to put mine across in a straightforward and practical way. As well as the detailed sections on how to improve your jumping, the book includes a chapter entitled 'Top Tips'. This aims to give easy, but effective, help and advice on all sorts of subjects – all based on knowledge acquired during a long riding career, which goes back to when I was seven years old. Although my parents were both non-horsey, they agreed to buy me a pony, a 12.2hh skewbald called Danny Boy. The big condition was that I had to do things properly and join the Pony Club.

My road to professional international show jumping therefore began with the Grove Hunt Branch. I threw myself into the games, rallies and summer camps. I took in the lessons about good horsemanship and listened to instruction on the care and welfare of our ponies. The Pony Club gave me excellent training – as well as good fun.

Nowadays, when I have become more involved in training, I get a great deal of satisfaction from seeing my riders achieve results. One thing that I tell each of them is that at the top level, riding skills alone are not enough: they must also have commitment, discipline, courage, resilience and focus. The golden rule is: 'There is no such word as "can't". You either will, or you won't.' As far as I am concerned, not to try is not an option.

Finally, I am proud that my elder son Joseph, aged five, is already a member of the Pony Club and enjoying light jumping and competitive games. I am sure he will get as much out of the Pony Club as I and so many others have done.

Happy, safe riding to all of you!

1
Introduction

Origins

The origins of the sport that we now call show jumping can be traced back some 150 years. It was in the middle of the 19th century when 'Leaping' competitions, designed to see how high or wide a horse could jump, first started to become popular. Before that the first recorded competitive equestrian event that featured any type of jumping at all had taken place in Ireland, in 1752, when a Mr O'Callaghan and a Mr Blake raced each other across country for four and a half miles, starting from the church at Buttevant, in Co Cork, and using the spire of the church at St Leger as a marker. This was the beginning of steeplechasing, though it would be another sixty years before specially designed courses were introduced, giving spectators the chance to watch the competitors' progress. Judging from the vivid portrayals by the sporting artists of the day, there was nothing very scientific about jumping at that time and a fair number of dramatic-looking falls were all too common.

Hunting and steeplechasing continued to be the sports for riders wishing to experience the thrills and spills of jumping until, in 1864, the first of two trial horse shows was held on Leinster Lawn in Dublin. Both shows included the High Jump and the Wide Leap, contests intended chiefly to test the qualifications of the horses in the hunter classes.

Two years later the French staged their first *concours hippique* (horse show) in Paris, and in 1868 the Royal Dublin Society launched its annual horse show, which is still going strong today. Both events included 'leaping' contests. In 1881 Belgium ran a *concours hippique* for the first time, and the famous National Horse Show in New York was inaugurated in 1883. The Dutch joined in three years later. High jumping and long jumping were included in the Olympic Games for the first time in Paris in 1900.

In those early days there were no courses as we know them today, just a handful of individual fences. There was no time limit and riders could virtually take as long as they wished getting their approach right for the next fence. There were no statutory rules and the most complicated scoring systems were invented, with different numbers of penalties being awarded for touching a fence or for knocking it down with either the forelegs or hind legs. At one time thin strips of wood known as laths (or 'slip fillets' in the United States) were placed along the tops of obstacles. Penalties were incurred for dislodging these, but fewer than for knocking down the fence itself; disputes often arose as to whether they had been knocked off by the horse or blown off by the wind. The stone wall which featured at the Royal Dublin Society show for many years had loose stones along the top and horses were penalised according to the number of stones they knocked off. Counting them must have been fun for the judges on a wet day!

Things had begun to take a more professional turn by 1909 when the third running of London's International Horse Show at Olympia included the world's first-ever show jumping Nations' Cup, and this was quickly followed by team events in Brussels, New York, Turin and Rome. A Nations' Cup was included at the Olympic Games for the first time in Stockholm in 1912. The sport of show jumping was well and truly on its way, though the governing international body, the FEI (*Fédération Equestre Internationale* or International Equestrian Federation) was not founded until 1921. Although in the early days team jumping was almost exclusively reserved for military riders, there were many talented civilians competing in the growing number of individual classes and, like most equestrian sports, jumping proved to be something at which women could compete on equal terms with men. The huge growth in the popularity of the sport is evident from the fact that today there are some 130 countries worldwide with national federations affiliated to the FEI.

Why go show jumping?

It is easy to understand why so many people, both riders and non-riders, enjoy show jumping. Unlike many other horse sports, it takes place in the confines of a not-too-large arena which makes it instantly accessible to spectators. Fans can see their equine and human heroes up close and follow their progress over every fence on the course. The scoring system is simple and competitions do not take all day. Nor is it just an outdoor summer sport. Nowadays, with top-level international meetings and much smaller national ones taking place indoors

Competing in style at the Pony Club Championships.

throughout the winter it is very much a round-the-year activity. For anyone wanting to take part, innumerable shows feature jumping classes for all abilities. The financial incentives may be negligible at the lower levels, but for those who achieve international success there are considerable rewards to be gained. And win or lose, there is always the fun of taking part. You don't even need to be a rider to be involved in this universally popular sport. Volunteering to help at local shows can be the first step towards greater things, such as stewarding or fence judging.

A little bit of bureaucracy

There are plenty of opportunities for newcomers to gain competitive experience. If you are under 21, you may join your local branch of the Pony Club, either as a member (up to the age of 18) or as an Associate Member (for those aged 18 to 21). All Pony Club branches organise a wide range of activities for members, and you will be able to benefit from both professional instruction and the chance to compete at a level appropriate to your skills. You don't necessarily need to have your own pony or horse, but can hire one from a riding school. The same applies to riding clubs, some of whom have wonderful facilities. Clubs are primarily designed for senior riders (17 and over), but some also accept junior members.

Pony Club competitions are an excellent preparation for the aspiring show jumper. Although they start at a very modest level they are, generally speaking, judged under the rules of the sport's national governing body, which in Britain is the British Show Jumping Association (BSJA). As well as rallies and summer camps run by branches, the Pony Club also organises junior/novice inter-branch competitions and, for the more advanced, area trials leading to the annual national team and individual championships.

If you wish to graduate from Pony Club classes to shows affiliated to the BSJA you will need to become a member of the Association, and your pony or horse must also be registered annually and the appropriate fees paid. Junior membership is available until the end of the calendar year in which you reach the age of 16 and gives you the right to compete as the rider of a pony in a competition affiliated to the BSJA. It also enables you to ride in a competition affiliated to the FEI or to any national federation which is a member of the FEI, subject to the rules and conditions for that particular competition.

As with the Pony Club, there is no lower age limit for junior members of the BSJA, but it is a condition of junior Association membership that someone in your immediate family, or a legally appointed guardian, must be a life, full or non-jumping BSJA member who will take responsibility for you and act on your behalf in all competitive matters, including the ownership of your ponies. If it is not possible for an immediate relative to do this, you can apply to the chief executive of the Association explaining why and nominate someone else who is a life or full member and who has agreed to act on your behalf.

Junior associate membership of the BSJA is available to those aged from 13 to16 and confers the right to ride either a pony or a horse at affiliated shows. This is particularly helpful for young people who have outgrown ponies. Those aged 17 to 18 may become associate members. The above age limits refer to the beginning of the year in which you reach the lower age (i.e. 13 or 17) and the end of the year in which you reach the upper age (i.e. 16 or 18). At the beginning of the year in which you celebrate your nineteenth birthday, you are entitled to become a full member of the Association.

The age limits for competing under FEI rules are somewhat different, pony classes being restricted to those aged from 12 to 16, juniors from 14 to 18 and young riders from 18 to 21. A young person cannot ride in a senior Grand Prix under FEI rules until they have reached their eighteenth year.

There are three height divisions under BSJA rules: ponies not exceeding 128cm, exceeding 128cm but not exceeding 138cm, and those standing 148cm or under. All measurements, incidentally, are taken without shoes. Any animal standing more than 148cm is classed as a horse.

Under BSJA rules, all ponies and horses are graded according to the amount of prize money they have won. A pony with no previous winnings enters affiliated jumping in grade JD. Once he has won a specified amount he becomes JC. Again, on reaching a higher, specified amount of prize money, he moves up to the top level, JA (there is no grade JB). These prize-money levels are reviewed periodically. With horses, the lowest grade is C, then B and finally A. Once a pony or horse has won an amount which places it in a higher grade, it cannot compete in competitions for which it is no longer eligible unless it competes *hors concours* (non-competitive).

Horses, even those standing only a fraction over 148cm, cannot compete in pony classes, but a pony may be registered in either the pony or horse grade appropriate to its total winnings in all grades. It is not unknown for exceptional ponies to successfully take on their larger brethren, right up to international level.

International championships

For the really ambitious rider there are various international championships, run under FEI rules, to aim for on the way up to senior level. If you and your pony are sufficiently successful, you might catch the eye of the British selectors and be invited to take part in a junior home pony international competition. Normally you would need to be partnering a JA pony to be in contention, though a particularly talented JC pony might also be considered. This is the first stepping stone to being groomed for a British pony team. The successful few might then progress to the junior team and then young riders. There are European Championships, with team and individual medals, at all three levels. Remember, however, that although these championships do provide invaluable experience and many international riders have competed in them on their way to the top, taking part is by no means the only way to succeed in show jumping.

2
Starting Out –
What You Need

Show jumping is an exhilarating sport that can be enjoyed by virtually anyone who rides. There are competitions to suit all ages and abilities and all sizes of horses and ponies. You certainly don't need a world-beating mount to enjoy taking part in shows. What you must remember, however, is that jumping is not a natural activity for a horse. Left to their own devices, horses who have not been taught to jump will almost always go round obstacles in their path rather than over them. It is important, therefore, if you and your horse are to enjoy show jumping and to do it effectively and safely, that both you and he learn the correct basic skills.

Correct jumping position

What type of horse do you need?

Clearly if you don't know how to ride over fences, you are not in a position to teach your horse, so if you have never jumped before, you should set out to find yourself a 'schoolmaster' horse or pony: one that has been doing the job with someone else. Good homes for such animals are always being sought, often because their previous riders have outgrown them or are perhaps about to concentrate full-time on their education. Usually a good home is more important to the person selling than the amount of money being asked. Remember that age is not really a barrier when you are setting out. Many ponies are very serviceable right up to and beyond the age of 20.

Begin by contacting members of your local Pony Club branch or riding club and putting the word about that you are looking for a pony or horse that is a competent jumper and would suit a novice rider. Recommendation by word of mouth is far better than trying to buy through advertisements. When you go to see a horse, always take along a knowledgeable person, someone who knows you and your capabilities. If you have been having lessons at a riding school, your instructor

A well-proportioned pony. Good feet and sound limbs are important, but don't be put off by the odd conformational defect. Jumping ability and a suitable temperament are more important than a handsome appearance.

would be an ideal person to ask; they can assess whether the horse is really going to be suitable for you. And don't be afraid to ask the owner lots of questions: what sort of bridle is he ridden in, is he good to shoe and clip, does he suffer from girth galls or saddle sores, does he chew his rugs, is he a good traveller? People are usually more than happy to be helpful. Watch him being ridden by a more experienced person and then ride and handle him yourself.

Although conformation is important, it isn't the be all and end all. Of course good feet are vital, as are sound limbs, with not too many lumps, bumps or scars. But look for a suitable temperament too. Certainly where ponies are concerned, conformational defects such as a ewe neck or a long back should not cause too much concern. If a pony is jumping successfully and doing his job well, then his track record and temperament are more important than his looks. He should be pleasant to handle, not too much of a live wire, not too sharp. Take note of his general behaviour and attitude. Is he well-mannered in the stable, is he happy to leave the yard on his own, does he seem willing to please when you ride him, will he work equally well in a group or alone? You will be spending a good deal of time in his company, so it is best if you choose an animal who is cooperative and fun to be with.

Remember, if you are planning to jump in affiliated competitions, that under BSJA rules horses and ponies are graded according to the amount of prize money they have won, and once they have moved up a grade they can no longer compete in lower grades. Don't, therefore, be tempted (even if you can afford it) to buy a successful Grade JA pony or Grade A horse when you are still a novice rider. Pony Club jumping competitions are open to various grades of ponies and horses but they must still be genuine Pony Club mounts and have participated in a designated number of working rallies. Be sure to familiarise yourself with the rules in advance.

Do you need help?
When you start to jump it is vital that you do so under the guidance of a qualified instructor – someone who can teach you the right techniques from the outset. Again, your local Pony Club branch or riding club will be able to help with names of suitable local people, or you could take a course of lessons at a reputable riding school. The British Horse Society and the Association of British Riding Schools both run approval schemes and it makes sense to choose a training centre that has this type of official recognition.

When booking lessons, remember that the more jumping you can do in a session the better. One good session is far better than lots of small ones. It is better to jump, say, 30 fences once a week than 10 fences three times a week because it is only by jumping plenty of fences that you begin to learn about timing and to build up your confidence. It is beneficial for the horse, too, not to be jumped every day. Jumping is quite hard work and a horse can end up damaging himself if he is over-jumped, especially if the ground is firm or very wet.

Quite apart from needing a coach to monitor your progress, it is very important from the point of view of safety that whenever you are jumping you have someone with you on the ground. Never be tempted to practise at home on your own. Safety aside, from the purely practical point of view you will of course also need someone to put jumps up for you and to move them around and generally be of assistance.

What facilities are necessary?

If you plan to have your own horse or pony and to keep him at home you will need a stable and somewhere secure to keep his tack; a paddock to turn him out in; a suitable area for riding (which can be a

portion of your paddock) and a supply of jumping poles and supports. For a pony, a loose-box should measure about 3.65m (12ft) by 3m (10ft). For a horse, it will need to be no smaller than 3.65m square.

You don't need a huge acreage to keep a horse – on average about an acre per horse (less for a pony) will be sufficient, provided you take good care of the pasture. What is essential for schooling purposes is an area of good, level ground free of ruts. This 'arena' should not be too small: there must be sufficient room for you to be able to get your horse cantering in a good flow and rhythm. It is important that the ground you jump on is neither very hard, nor soft and loose. It should be soft enough not to produce concussion when the horse jumps, but it should not move away under his feet when he takes off – if it does he might frighten himself. When jumping on wet grass, always fit studs in his shoes to give him sufficient grip.

When building your practice fences it is very important to use proper show jumping poles and supports, not left-over planks of wood from a building site. All wood used for constructing fences must be free of splinters to avoid causing injury to horse or rider, or indeed to any-one handling the jumps. Some people use old oil drums as supports but these have a metal lip around the top which can be quite dangerous.

Left and above *For practice purposes always use proper show jumping poles and supports.*

19

Machined poles and jump-stands with correctly fitted safety cups for the poles to rest on are by far the safest.

If you don't have your own facilities, or if you have insufficient time to care for a horse on a daily basis, you could consider keeping him at livery, that is pay for him to live at someone else's yard. Full livery can prove quite an expensive option, though you can bring the charges down if you opt for part livery and do some of the daily work (say mucking out and/or grooming) yourself. On the plus side, you could benefit considerably from being able to use any training facilities which the yard has, such as a proper jumping arena with a good all-weather surface. There is also the advantage of having expert help on hand should you need it.

If you are unable to have your own horse or pony, don't be down-hearted. There is no reason why you can't learn to jump at your local riding school or branch of the Pony Club on a borrowed mount and then have fun competing in the shows that these organisations run.

Everyday equipment

Safety and comfort are paramount whether you are jumping or riding on the flat so it is best always to wear clothes designed for the purpose. Although you can wear jeans with a pair of chaps, jodhpurs or breeches tend to be more comfortable. Always wear boots specifically designed for riding, i.e. with a small heel that cannot slip through the stirrup-iron, and a hat made to the latest safety specification. The harness should be correctly adjusted and you should wear it fastened whenever you are mounted. Gloves tend to be a matter of preference, though they can be very helpful in wet weather. There are lots of good ones on the market designed to give extra grip.

Tack

A lot of emphasis is placed on the type of saddle you choose for jumping, but a good quality bridle is just as important – perhaps even more so. It must fit the horse comfortably if he is to do his job satisfactorily. As for bits, it is always best to try to keep things simple – many horses go perfectly well in a plain snaffle. Always opt for easy-grip reins, since leather ones aren't great for show jumping if the horse gets sweaty or if the weather is wet. Continental-style reins or those fitted with rubber grips are best.

A running martingale is a very useful aid for the show jumper, particularly for the less experienced rider, since it gives stability and definition to the ride. A horse cannot evade the bridle so easily and is less likely to make the sort of sloppy turn you often see, where the horse turns his head in the required direction but not his body. To ride a horse well without a martingale you have to be softer and more skilled in your ride.

There are any number of excellent jumping saddles on the market but they can be expensive and there is certainly no need to invest in one to begin with. It is perfectly possible to show jump at the lower levels in a good general-purpose saddle. Obviously, care must be taken that it fits both the horse and you. It mustn't in any way press on the horse's withers or backbone and it must be cut in such a way that you are able to shorten your stirrups sufficiently for jumping. Girths are put

Keep things simple: most horses go perfectly well in a plain snaffle. Easy-grip reins are advisable and a running martingale is a useful aid for the less experienced rider.

Care must be taken that the saddle fits both horse and rider. Always use good quality girths, stirrup-leathers and irons.

under great stress when a horse is jumping, so choose good quality ones. Wide girths will be more comfortable for the horse than narrow ones, which are likely to pinch.

Always use strong, good quality stirrup-leathers and stainless steel stirrup-irons. The latter should be large enough to provide a gap of about 1.25cm (½in) either side of your foot. Never use irons that are so large that your foot could easily slip through, or so small that your foot could become trapped if you were to fall off.

Check all your tack regularly, especially the stitching. Remember that jumping puts a good deal of strain on items such as girths and stirrup leathers. Don't run the risk of something giving way while you are riding.

If you have a horse or pony who really snaps up his front legs when he jumps, you may find that he is inclined to strike into himself with his jumping studs. To prevent this you can fit a stud-guard on his girths. Stud-guards are expensive and are in no way a necessity for all horses and ponies but if there is a real risk of injury it is well worth investing in one.

By using a numnah and saddle-pad under your saddle you can help reduce the concussion on the horse's back when he jumps. A squarer type of numnah with a saddle-pad underneath works well. Try to avoid pads and numnahs which come so far down the horse's sides that they tend to push your leg away from the horse.

Always fit tendon boots in front and fetlock boots behind when you are jumping, whether you are competing or just schooling at home. When horses are learning to jump, their legs tend to go all over the place and it's so easy for them to strike into themselves. A set of boots is a great deal cheaper than a vet's fee! Open-fronted boots are best for show jumpers since they encourage a horse to be more careful. If you wrap protective pads right round a horse's legs, he might be inclined to

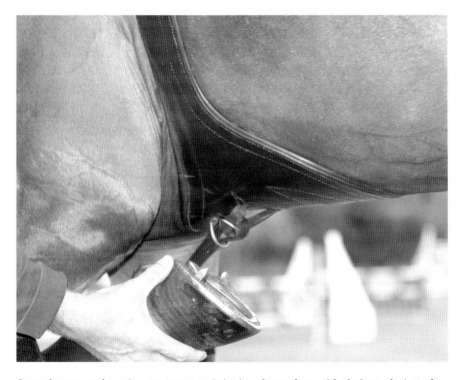

Some horses and ponies are prone to injuring themselves with their studs. A stud guard, fitted to the girths, will prevent this.

23

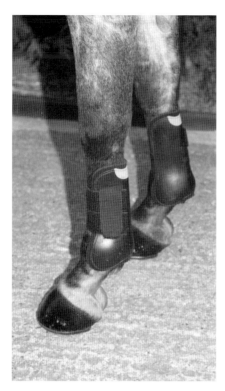 

Two types of tendon boots: left, plastic boots with Velcro fastenings; right, leather boots with straps and buckles.

be less careful, knowing that he won't feel it if he gives a pole a knock. Always fit overreach boots when jumping in deep going.

Studs

Studs, which help to prevent a horse from slipping, are a vital piece of equipment when jumping on grass. There are different types of stud to suit different types of going. As a general rule you should only be jumping in good conditions, when the ground is not too hard or too deep; but conditions are not always perfect, so be prepared. Jumping-studs, which screw into holes provided in the horse's shoes by the farrier, give the horse more purchase and therefore more confidence, preventing him from slipping when going into his fences and when turning.

Pointed studs give the best purchase when the ground is dry and on the hard side. Bigger, squarer studs are needed when the ground is wet. Allow for a minimum of two studs per shoe, or even three for the back shoes. If you do use three behind, two should be in the back heel of the shoe and the third should be located on the quarter clip.Remove the studs after jumping and protect the screw holes by plugging them with oiled cotton wool. Check them regularly and replug them. If the screw threads are damaged, you won't be able to fit the studs again.

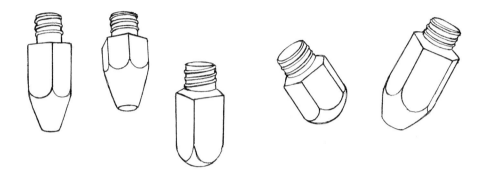

Jumping studs come in a variety of shapes. Pointed studs give the best purchase when the ground is dry. In wet conditions you should use big, square studs.

3
The Basic Techniques

Before you begin to learn how to ride over fences, it is important to understand exactly what the horse is doing when he is jumping. The first thing to bear in mind is that he is first and foremost a perfectly designed galloping machine. He is built with his 'engine' at the rear to enable him to move fast by pushing himself forwards. Nature did not intend him to go upwards; however, if we want him to jump, this is exactly what we need him to do. Compare the horse with, say, a kangaroo and you will see the difference between an animal designed to run and one designed to jump. Instead of the horse's rather straight back legs, the kangaroo has back legs that are more Z-shaped. Whereas the horse has a heavy front end – large shoulders, long front legs, long neck and heavy head – the kangaroo has very narrow shoulders, small 'arms', a short neck and small head. His body broadens down to a very

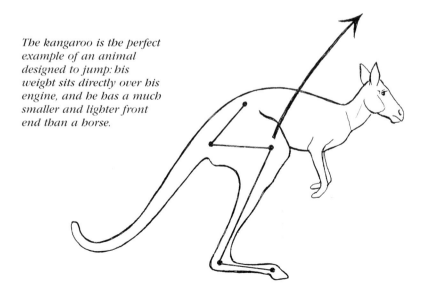

The kangaroo is the perfect example of an animal designed to jump: his weight sits directly over his engine, and he has a much smaller and lighter front end than a horse.

bulky lower half. Unlike the horse, his weight sits directly above his engine so that he is spring-like not only in shape but also in effect. To gain forward momentum he simply inclines his body forward.

In order to create a jumping creature out of our galloping horse we need to pick up his body, as it were, and put it on to his bottom, kangaroo-fashion. This, in fact, is what happens when he jumps. When he reaches a fence, a correctly trained horse puts in a nice round stride, pats the ground with his front feet and immediately adjusts his balance in a backward movement so that his engine is directly below the rest of his body weight. Only then can he push himself upwards.

In – Back – Upwards – Forwards: these are the critical movements which a horse must make in order to jump successfully, forwards being the last movement of all. It is vitally important when training horses to jump to give them the time to what we call 'prop', that is to go in, back and up. If you ride your horse with too much pace and too much speed he will jump off his front feet and will land more strongly, more running, than when he took off. On the other hand, he will land more steeply and more softly if he is given time to use his body in a bascule – a word derived from the French to seesaw and used to describe the curling shape which a well-trained horse makes over the top of a fence, with his shoulders being the highest point and his head and neck stretching forwards. This technique is similar to that used by a high-jumper. Although the human athlete does it backwards, he too flicks his

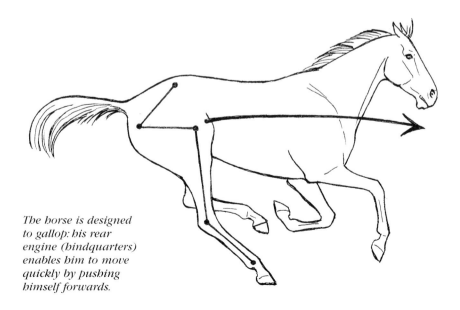

The horse is designed to gallop: his rear engine (hindquarters) enables him to move quickly by pushing himself forwards.

legs and curls round the bar. As with the high-jumper, the better the horse's bascule, the less effort he has to make to clear the fence.

The rider's position

It is vitally important to learn control and good balance on the flat before you even begin to think about jumping. You must be competent at walk, trot and canter, and be able to perform smooth upward and downward transitions – i.e. going up from walk to trot to canter, and coming back from canter to trot to walk. Some riders are very keen to start jumping before they are ready. This can be dangerous and you may end up hurting yourself. Remember that the correct techniques not only make jumping safer, they also make it more enjoyable for both horse and rider.

Because the horse has to balance not only himself but also your weight when he jumps, it is vital that your centre of gravity should be as close as possible to his to enable him to do the job efficiently. Your position in the approach to a fence, at the moment of take-off, in flight over the fence, during the landing and the getaway stride is therefore of great importance.

When jumping it is crucial always to have a vertical stirrup leather. By having a straight line through the stirrup leather you bring your weight into your heel, lessening the weight on your seat and putting it more on your lower leg, as a result of which you bring your centre of gravity closer to that of the horse. You should have an open shoulder and create an L-shape from your elbow to the reins. This helps you achieve a good constant contact with the horse, enabling you to give

The correct rider position: note the L-shape from the arm to the reins and the vertical stirrup leather.

29

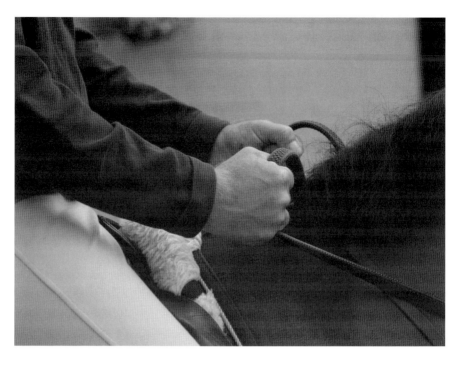

Hands to avoid: the fist (above) and the sloppy (below).

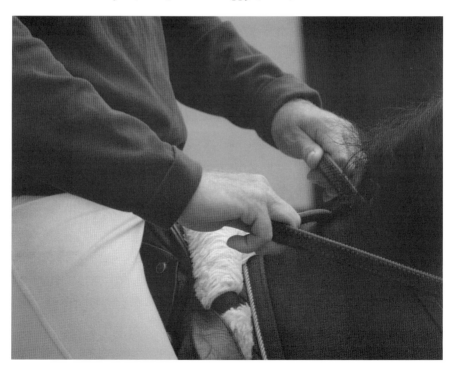

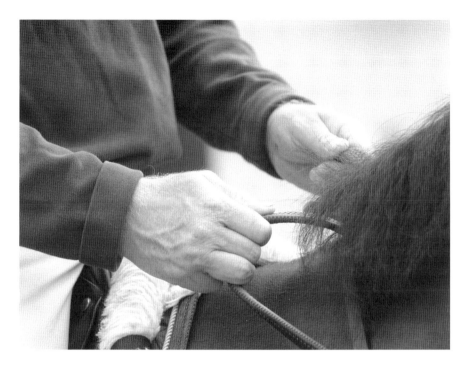

Your hands should be solid and positive but with open fingers which will give you the right contact with your horse.

and take with his movements. It is essential to avoid blocking up the top half of your body by having too straight an arm position. Your hand position should be solid and positive but with open fingers that will create the feel you need in order to have a good contact with your horse. Your hand should not be a fist, which will create tension, but neither should it be in a sloppy, 'wet-fish' position. Think in terms of a handshake – not so hard that it hurts, not so soft that it gives the wrong impression. Positive but elastic hands will help your horse to become more relaxed in his head carriage.

On the approach to a fence you should be sitting in balance with your horse, not stiffly but 'living with the movement', and looking where you are going. On the last stride before take-off (not the actual take-off itself) you must soften your shoulders, gently allowing them to go towards the horse's head. At the moment of take-off, you need to stand up slightly in your stirrups to take your weight out of the saddle. You shouldn't throw your body forwards, but just release your seat. By releasing your seat you put your weight in your heel and by putting your weight in your heel you maintain a more solid leg position,

The correct way to jump: a balanced approach is followed by a releasing of the seat at the moment of take-off.

The solid lower leg position ensures that the rider stays in balance throughout the jump. The hands maintain a positive but elastic contact. The seat is still out of the saddle as the horse lands.

therefore making it a lot easier to stay in balance over the fence. This release of the seat means that the horse can use his whole back. You should keep your head up and look where you're going at all times.

As the horse lands, your seat should still be slightly out of the saddle. On the impact of landing, your knees should act as shock absorbers, then on the first stride away from the fence, you should regain your position by sitting up tall in the saddle. As the horse lands you should 'soak' – that is absorb the impact of landing throughout your whole body – then sit, not land and sit bolt upright, which produces concussion through the saddle to the horse's back. This might well make him shoot away from the fence.

Some people advise riders to grab hold of a piece of mane when they first begin to jump. This is not a good idea because it teaches you to rest on your hands, and before you know it you will be resting on your hands every time you jump rather than releasing your seat. The way to maintain balance is to lessen the weight on your seat by putting it through the lower leg, which in turn produces the required solid lower leg position.

Too many riders are told to go forwards into the jumping position. If

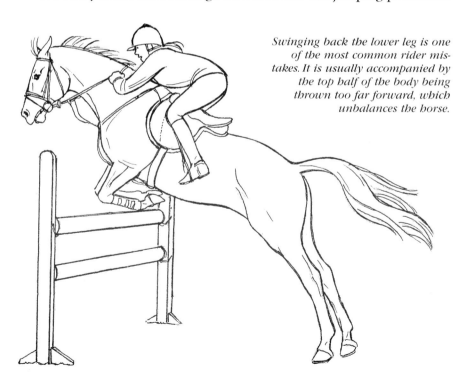

Swinging back the lower leg is one of the most common rider mistakes. It is usually accompanied by the top half of the body being thrown too far forward, which unbalances the horse.

you do this, your body weight will be thrown forwards which is in direct contradiction to what the horse should be doing – that is coming back on to his hocks. Rather than folding from the tummy, which is what many people are taught, always think 'release the seat'.

One of the most common mistakes is to swing back your lower leg. This probably means that the top half of your body is being thrown too far forward. Or you may be gripping only with your knees, whereas there should be contact with the saddle from mid-calf right through to mid-thigh. If you body goes too far forwards, you may have to put your hands out to maintain balance, which in turn means that the horse has to adjust his balance. The chances are that it will pitch him on to his front end and make him very elongated.

Basic flatwork

The show jumper needs to be soft and supple through his head and neck, and through his back. When you are walking your horse around before a schooling session, ask him to flex gently to the left; then to the right; left and then right; and so on. You should not need to move your whole body when doing this. If you do, it will illustrate how stiff your horse has become. Then ask him to do a little leg yielding, that is to move away from your leg on both reins. Little things like this help you when jumping a course because they enable you to support and balance your horse through his turns.

It is essential for the show jumper to trot in balance, not leaning on or running into your hands. You should not have to work too hard to support the horse. Light contact should always be there but he should maintain his rhythm and his own balance. Always work on both reins, changing the diagonals regularly, and remember that rising trot helps a horse to use his back.

A good canter is of great importance to the show jumper. It must be balanced and even. It should be 'in a cog', that is the horse should be able to maintain his canter without assistance from the rider. Too many riders have to keep telling their horses to stay in canter. It is hard work and a horse becomes very dull from the leg if the rider is forever kick, kick, kicking. Your leg should always be in contact with the horse, but one instruction to canter should be sufficient. Thereafter, allow him to stay in his own canter, allow the rhythm to develop. What will happen is that the horse will start to hold himself. If he breaks into trot, ask him to canter again straight away. Say 'I didn't ask you to trot' and he will

Opposite *Work on the flat helps to make the horse soft and supple.*

Above *The show jumper must be able to trot in balance. Trotting over poles (square ones are safer than round ones) helps to improve his rhythm and balance.*

A good, balanced canter is vital for the show jumper. He should maintain his canter without the need for continual kicking from the rider.

soon understand and say 'Oh, I see, I've got to keep cantering until you tell me to stop'. this is a lot easier than constantly having to tell him to keep cantering.

It is a misconception to think that you should have to do all the work. Horses are bigger and stronger than us – they are, after all, work horses. If we as riders do a bit less, it's amazing how much they will do for us. Once the horse is holding his canter and remaining more balanced, the rider can do less and maintain a better, softer position; riding then becomes more pleasurable.

The first jump

The best way to begin is to ride over a raised pole at a rising trot, a pace that is more manageable than a canter. The pole need be no more than 4 or 5 inches (10 or 12.5cms) off the ground. Start with one, then build up to two, then three, in a row, with two strides between each.

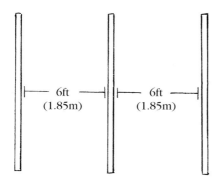

Before you attempt to jump a fence, practise trotting over raised poles.

For your first attempt at jumping a fence, build a small cross-pole, no more than 1ft (30cm) high. A cross-pole encourages a horse to jump right at the centre of the fence. It also looks bigger than it actually is and so encourages him to try harder. Place a plank on the ground in front of it; for a horse approaching at trot, the plank should be 7½ft (2.3m) in front of the fence, for a pony 6½ft (2m). When you come to approach at canter you will need to bring the plank a little further out, to 10ft (3m) for a horse, 8½ft (2.6m) for a pony.

The reason for using a plank is that it creates a rounder stride just before take-off. Because the trot is a two-time movement, with the legs working in diagonal pairs, asking a horse to jump a fence from trot is like trying to teach a person to play football with one leg tied up. The plank makes the horse use his two front feet and two back feet together to create a balanced jump over the little fence. This is often

Trotting to a plank placed on the ground in front of a small cross-pole fence is the ideal way to get started. The plank creates a rounder stride.

The plank on the ground encouraged the horse to form a good curved shape or bascule.

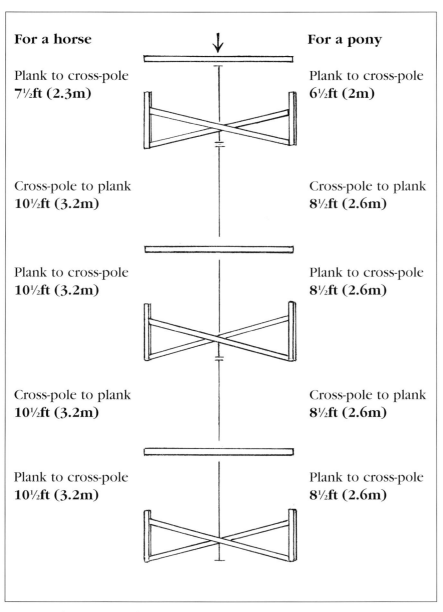

For a horse

Plank to cross-pole
7½ft (2.3m)

Cross-pole to plank
10½ft (3.2m)

Plank to cross-pole
10½ft (3.2m)

Cross-pole to plank
10½ft (3.2m)

Plank to cross-pole
10½ft (3.2m)

For a pony

Plank to cross-pole
6½ft (2m)

Cross-pole to plank
8½ft (2.6m)

Plank to cross-pole
8½ft (2.6m)

Cross-pole to plank
8½ft (2.6m)

Plank to cross-pole
8½ft (2.6m)

Distances for an approach at trot.

Practise the canter approach by placing a plank on the ground in front of a small cross-pole and let the rhythm take you to the fence.

referred to as a 'placing pole' but I prefer to think of it more as creating a good round stride at the fence. A plank, painted white or striped, is preferable to a round pole; if the horse treads on a pole it might roll away, trip him up and cause injury, whereas a plank will not. If you don't have planks, use a square pole which won't roll.

When you can ride over the plank and cross-pole confidently and in balance, put another plank on the ground on the landing side, approximately 10ft (3m) away from the fence. When the horse takes off he will look down and see the plank and it will make him form a good curved shape over the fence – a bascule. Now add a second fence one non-jumping stride from the first. Bearing in mind that the average non-jumping canter stride for a horse is 12ft (3.65m) and for a pony 10ft (3m), and allowing half a stride (6ft or 1.83m for a horse, 5ft or 1.52m for a pony) for landing and half a stride for take-off, this means that the distance between the two fences should be about 24ft or 7.3m (20ft or 6m for a pony), though when riding at trot you will need to reduce this a little, to about 21ft (6.4m) (17ft or 5.2m for a pony). As before, approach the plank in front of the first fence at a good rising trot. Once you can ride over the two fences in balance, add a third.

Approaching a fence at canter

The mistake many riders make when they first approach a fence at canter is to start looking for the take-off distance instead of allowing the horse's rhythm to get them to the fence. They almost fire the horse at the jump and as a result he lands running and out of balance. Let the rhythm take you, and the take-off distance from the fence will be correct. Since the take-off distance is half a horse's stride and the distance for landing the same, the actual jump is simply an exaggerated stride. Remember that the more you alter the horse's stride pattern, the more likely you are to get an unbalanced jump. The more regular you can keep the horse's stride, the more balanced it will be and the more the jump will be a natural progression from that. Rhythm is the main ingredient in jumping. Allow the fence to come to you, do not attack it, maintain the horse's rhythm and let him concentrate on the fence.

Always maintain contact over the jump, albeit a light, elastic contact;

Rhythm over fences

Cantering over poles, either on the ground or raised a few inches above it, improves a horse's stride pattern.

as it is your main way of communicating with the horse it would be silly to throw it away. But your hands mustn't become stiff or heavy or hard. Keep your head up and maintain your balance through your lower leg position: too many riders make it complicated; simplicity is best. A good craftsman always makes a job look easy.

The important thing with jumping is not to try to run before you can walk. Your confidence must be bubbling over. Not until you can jump three fences in a row, with one or two strides in between, and can maintain balance over all three, should you start thinking about jumping a small course. Up to then, it is better to keep practising down a line or 'grid' in order to perfect your balance and timing.

Improving the canter

All too often horses are asked to trot round a school for hours but are never asked to hold their canter for more than one or two circuits. Yet, as we have seen, a sustained, balanced canter is vital to the show jumper. A good way of improving a horse's canter and teaching you to be aware of his stride pattern is to ride over raised poles. Having to negotiate these small jumps 'lifts' the canter. To begin with, set three poles along each of the long sides of your school - allow 12ft (3.65m) between each pole for a horse, 10ft (3m) for a pony. Practise cantering over these raised poles until your horse can sustain a good, round canter. Eventually, you can remove the middle one so that he is having to canter further between the poles but is still holding his canter.

Jumping a small course

Jumping a course is obviously more difficult than jumping fences in a straight line. To jump a course successfully you must be able to maintain a good-quality balanced canter, not too fast, not too slow, not too long,

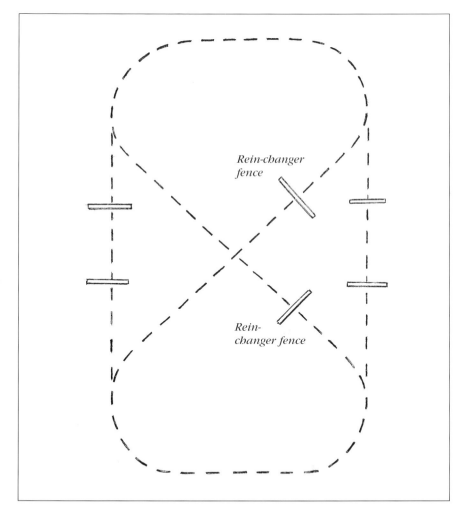

Allow no more than 4 or 5 horse strides between the fences on the long sides of the arena.

not too short. You must thread the whole of your course around the theory of rhythm and how it helps the horse to be more balanced and more accurate. And you must keep your horse on a smooth line, avoiding very sharp, angular turns. Remember that your horse doesn't have a hinge in the middle. Your lines don't always have to be straight, but they must be smooth – never leave your turns too late. Keep your instructions simple and as soon as you have taken off at one fence, start concentrating on the next one.

To begin with, a simple course in a tight figure-of-eight will suffice: two small fences on the right rein, then a fence on the diagonal to change the rein, then two fences on the left rein and finally another rein-changer on the diagonal. To ensure that your horse stays controllable, keep the distances between the two fences on the long sides of the arena short, no more than four or five horse strides; the longer the distance between fences the more room there is for the horse to become bigger in his stride pattern and therefore slightly out of control. At this stage all six fences should be small uprights. This is not only easy for the horse but it also means that you will need less equipment. Practise over this little course several times, but no more than five or six times in one jumping session.

A small spread fence is no harder to jump than a vertical. The groundline, provided by the pole on the floor, makes it easier for the horse.

There is a little rhyme which I like to use when I am training:

REMEMBER: CANTER – RHYTHM — LINE
GETS IT RIGHT EVERY TIME
- Always aim for a good quality **CANTER**
- Maintain the horse's **RHYTHM**.
- Keep your **LINE** direct –always let the horse know where he is going.

Changing the rein

It is really important when jumping a course for the horse to be on the correct canter lead at all times so that he stays in balance. The rein-changer fences on the little figure-of-eight course are there to help you to feel the change of rein. If when you land over the rein-changer fence the horse is on the wrong leg for the next turn, you should come back to trot and ask him to strike off again on the correct leg. This is one of the occasions when having someone on the ground to help you is so useful, since they can tell you if you land on the wrong leg.

A good way of practising the change of rein is to make a serpentine in your school (with minimum diameters of 65ft or 20m), using wings without poles. Riding the serpentine alternately trotting, cantering, trotting, cantering will give you the idea of the rein changes without having to jump. You can then put poles on the ground between the wings and go over those. Finally, build them up to raised poles or small fences.

Jumping spread fences

A spread fence, certainly up to intermediate level – 1.10m – is primarily designed as a rider frightener and does not need to be ridden any differently from a vertical. As we have already seen, an average horse's stride is 12ft (3.65m) so a fence with a spread of 3ft (0.91cm) is equivalent to a quarter of a horse's stride – in human terms only the equivalent of a 9in (22.5cm) puddle that we might gently step over. You wouldn't need to take a run-up for that, would you? So there is no need to ride more strongly, with more speed, to a small spread fence than there is to a vertical. When practising over spread fences, however, it is a good idea when you make the spread a little wider to rest one end of the far pole on the edge of the cup, rather than placing it in it, so that if the horse does make a mistake the pole will fall directly. This means that if things do go wrong the horse cannot injure himself and you will be more relaxed knowing that you are not going to become suspended or to trip the horse up.

4

Developing and Improving

To succeed in show jumping a rider must have 'feel'. In fact, 'feel' is a very big part of all riding. Watch the top internationals in action and even though you may spot certain flaws in their technique you will soon recognise the empathy they have with their horses. Creating that empathy is a vital part of training, and learning to 'feel' the horse's stride is the single most important aspect. When you are riding, the horse's legs should, as it were, become your legs, the horse's brain your brain. When you can marry the two you will find that jumping becomes a great deal easier.

There are various exercises to help promote this feel for the stride in both rider and horse. Try building a cross-pole fence and then marking out four or five horse strides on the landing side by placing poles on the ground at 12ft (3.65m) intervals, that is one horse-stride apart – for ponies 10ft (3m) intervals. Practise over these repeatedly, counting the strides aloud. Then remove all but the last pole and ride over the fence and this one pole, still counting the strides aloud. You will find that through repetition the definition of the stride is still there even though the 'stepping stones' have been removed. It is rather like having a tune in your mind which you cannot get rid of. You can then replace the remaining pole with a small fence. When you land over the cross-pole you should be able to feel the strides just as you could when you were using the poles. In other words, your brain will be linked with the horse's movement.

Grids and gridwork

Gridwork, or gymnastic jumping as it is also known, is an important part of training for both horse and rider. Working over a line of poles and small jumps – with distances of one, two or three horse strides between – promotes athleticism, suppleness and balance in the horse. It develops the correct shape, technique and regularity of stride which are all essential for successful show jumping. Once you and your horse are coping successfully with simple grids you can begin work over bounces – that is, grids which do not allow the horse to take a stride between the fences. Bounce grids not only help to make a horse more athletic throughout his body, they also stimulate his mind.

Gridwork of all kinds is also highly beneficial for the rider, since it helps you to develop a sense of timing and a more consistent rhythm and stride pattern. It puts structure into your riding and takes out the inconsistencies.

The ultimate grid

This grid has all the ingredients required to teach your horse both the correct jumping techniques and also the right thought processes. Begin by placing a square pole on the ground followed by one cross-pole fence. Then add a second fence – a small single rail with a pole as a groundline – about 10½ ft (3.2m) from the first to create a bounce. For a pony place the second fence 8½ft (2.6m) from the first. The idea of the bounce is to encourage the horse to use his shoulders and front end, to develop the bascule and to create forward momentum. As soon as he lands over the first cross-pole he has to take off again immediately, his shoulders acting as the lever for his body rather than his back end where he normally gets his power from. Distance-wise, a bounce is simply a landing and a take-off added together, that is half a stride for landing and half a stride for take-off. We know that the required distance for that is 12ft (3.65m) for a horse, 10ft (3m) for a pony, but in this exercise we need to shorten the distance a little to ensure that the horse works his front end.

Next, add a square pole on the ground followed by a small spread fence. After the bounce the horse must balance himself and make a good round shape over the pole on the ground. He then has to prop, moving his body weight back on to his hocks in order to jump the parallel. When he has done this a couple of times, increase the height of the spread fence and make it wider by shortening the take-off distance (i.e. bring the front part of the fence forwards). This will encourage the horse to come back even more on to his hocks.

The beauty of this grid is that it tests the horse in all departments. He has to think for himself and use his technique because the grid is built in such a way that he cannot use power to go forwards, he has to use

The ultimate grid (1): a square pole on the ground is followed by a cross-pole fence. After jumping the cross-pole the horse must bounce the little vertical.

The ultimate grid (2): when the horse lands over the bounce fence he must make a good round shape over the pole on the ground, prop and jump the parallel.

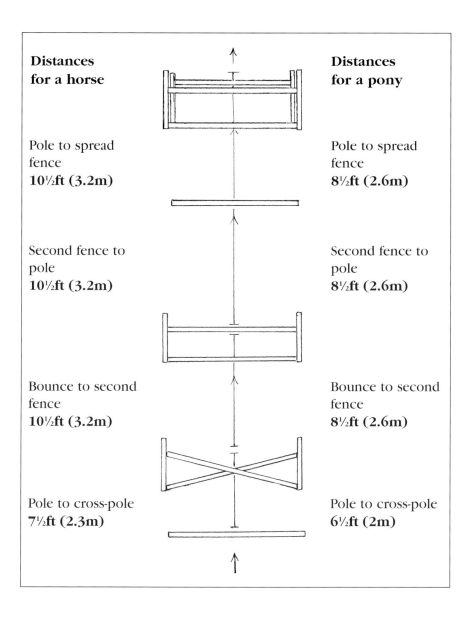

Distances for a horse

Pole to spread fence
10½ft (3.2m)

Second fence to pole
10½ft (3.2m)

Bounce to second fence
10½ft (3.2m)

Pole to cross-pole
7½ft (2.3m)

Distances for a pony

Pole to spread fence
8½ft (2.6m)

Second fence to pole
8½ft (2.6m)

Bounce to second fence
8½ft (2.6m)

Pole to cross-pole
6½ft (2m)

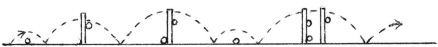

The ultimate grid teaches the horse the correct jumping techniques and the right thought processes. It comprises a pole on the ground, followed by a cross-pole fence and a bounce to a small vertical. Another pole on the ground makes the horse balance himself and make a good round shape over the final spread fence.

power to go upwards. It encourages him to take a round stride going in, to use his shoulders through the bounce, to take another round stride after the bounce and to come back and push himself higher and harder over the spread fence. We are therefore getting our horse to do everything that we require within a jump: the correct shape, the stride, the prop and the power.

As a rider, it is imperative for you to be with the horse, not against him, when riding this grid. Remember that it is impossible to sit to the movement of the bounce. And don't sit up with your body over the obstacles because that will prevent the horse from going forwards. You must allow your knees to act as shock absorbers. It is important not to come in too fast and not to sit up too early on landing. Sit up gently. Remember, too, that keeping your head up will help you to maintain your balance.

Advanced gridwork: multiple bounces

A multiple-bounce grid is a good exercise for encouraging a horse to work his front end and to develop the round stride pattern. It is also a good position-exercise for the rider, who must maintain balance throughout the grid. From the safety point of view it is best to use diagonally slanting poles when building bounce grids, in other words small fences consisting of a pole with one end resting on the support cup and the other on the ground. If you jump multiple bounces with poles suspended in the normal way, with each end in a cup, the horse is more likely to be brought down should he make a mistake. With slanting poles if there is a problem, all the horse has to do to get out of trouble is to go towards the low side of the pole. The other benefit of using alternate slanting poles is that they challenge the horse optically. He has to use his brain to interpret the puzzle in front of him.

Begin by placing a pole on the ground 7½ft (2.3m) for a horse, or 6½ft (2m) for a pony from a cross-pole fence, followed by one slanting-pole fence at a distance of 10½ft (3.2m) for a horse, 8½ft (2.6m) for a pony. Use this shorter distance rather than 12ft (3.65m) for a horse, 10ft (3m) for a pony, in order to really define the bounce. Decide on which rein you are going to approach, and place the raised end of the first diagonal-pole fence on the opposite side. This will encourage the horse to finish his turn and then to stay straight. As soon as he lands over the cross-pole fence he will create a jump over the slanting pole from his front end. Since his back end will still be in the air, your seat must be off the saddle and you must as always allow your knees and legs to act as shock absorbers. Rider balance is crucial, as is contact with the horse's head. Don't throw the contact away. If you do the horse will go down the grid out of balance.

Next, add a third obstacle, that is, a second bounce. Put the high end of the pole on the opposite side to that of the first bounce pole. As the horse comes to the grid he will immediately see all the poles and, because his focus is different from yours, he will not be able to focus on the bounce poles until he is landing over the cross-pole. As he goes down the grid it will begin to become clear to him, but it requires a degree of faith in you as a rider when he first begins to jump this type of grid. Should he start to panic, don't be afraid to take out the last-bounce and go back a step in order to regain his trust and confidence. Only then should you continue adding to the grid.

When you start riding over the two bounce poles you will begin to feel the horse moving slightly from left to right and back to left again. He will be starting to think about what he is doing with his body. As with any athlete, when he gains control of his body he will be able to use himself better. Once he is going over the cross pole and two bounces confidently, add a third bounce, again with the pole slanting the opposite way from the one before. The more bounces you add, the more information the horse has to take in, so don't just keeping building up and up until he starts to panic. Keep him soft and relaxed and remember to give him a breather regularly. This exercise puts quite a lot of strain on the horse's front legs, because when he lands he has to take off immediately, using his forearms instead of his back legs. Confidence is the key in such a complicated grid and you must be receptive at all times to what your horse is telling you.

To begin with he might tend to run on a little, in other words he might over-exaggerate the forward momentum. If you feel him doing this, concentrate on coming in softly and making sure that you keep your contact. Ask him not to get too big and forward. With practice he will learn to balance himself and develop a good bascule technique. This is where this grid pays dividends: it teaches a horse to be in control of his body and his balance.

When the horse is coping well with three bounces, add a fourth, that is obstacle number 5. But be aware that it is when you get to four, five or six bounces that horses are most likely to start panicking. If you feel him doing so, go back to the previous level for a while longer. Don't be greedy, don't go for too much in one go. It will take practice for your

Advanced gridwork: the multiple-bounce grid encourages the horse to use himself both physically and mentally.

The more bounces you add to the grid, the more information the horse has to take in. This is a complicated exercise and you should build it up slowly to prevent him from panicking.

horse to become relaxed with so many bounces in a row. He will really have to think. Be patient, be sure to keep nice and straight, off the seat, and remember to change the rein regularly. And don't forget to praise your horse when he does well.

Once you have built up to six bounces, the horse will be having to work quite hard. You'll feel him beginning to weave his body down the line. All being well, your balance will still be in tune with his, you will be maintaining your jumping position and your knees will be acting as shock absorbers.

Shortening the distance between fences

After riding the bounce grid it is a good idea to move on immediately to a very short one-stride double. This is because the horse needs to be able to make the distinction between a bounce and a one-stride distance. Build a double with cross-poles set 18ft (5.47m) apart for a horse, 15ft (4.54m) for a pony that is with one half-stride between the two elements. In order to impress the horse, use a flat plank on the ground in the middle. Use quite large cross-pole fences in order to impress the horse. We want our horses to think, to be mentally challenged. It is not really the height of the fences that we are working on here, it is the development of his skills to help him to make the right decisions. A big cross-pole looks impressive but is still a very simple fence to jump. Remember that the horse has just been doing bounces, so don't come into the double too forward. Be disciplined and wait a little. If you see a long stride, don't go on it. Using this double directly after the bounce grid makes a horse use his brain. It stimulates him mentally, which in turn helps prepare him for the challenges he will face when competing.

When he is jumping the double confidently, add a third part, making this last cross-pole the biggest. Again this will challenge the horse mentally, although when he actually jumps the fences he will find them a lot easier than they appeared at first. This all helps to build his confidence. It is so important for the training not only to give you and your horse skills, but also to pour confidence into the horse so that when he comes to go into the jumping ring he feels as if he can do the job.

By having three cross-poles in a row on very short distances, we are telling the horse that he must back up, use his technique and be soft, not aggressive, at his fences. Following on from the bounce work, which made the horse use himself and become supple through his back, this type of

Three cross-poles on very short distances teach a horse to be soft, not aggressive at his fences. They challenge him mentally and help to build his confidence.

exercise teaches the horse to think correctly, to make a choice. He learns to look at the puzzle, work it out and come to a successful conclusion.

Related distances

Once you have learnt to feel the stride, once your brain is married to the horse's movement, you can learn to ride related distances. Two fences that have no fewer than three strides and no more than seven strides between them are said to be on a related distance. Because they are so close together, the way you jump the first will have an impact on the way you jump the second. Related distances cause problems for many riders, though there is no reason why they should, as long as you know how to walk these distances accurately and that you ride them with the correct stride pattern. What you must remember is that the course designer is building for the average horse. He is not going to change things because your horse happens to take a big or a small stride.

How to walk a related distance

Before you can walk related distances accurately you need to learn how to take even one-yard strides, bearing in mind that four human strides equal one average stride of the horse at canter. Begin by laying a standard 12ft (3.65m) jumping pole on the ground (measure it to make sure that it is exactly 12ft) then practise walking alongside it until you can walk from end to end in four even strides. To start with, look down to check the distance as you go and try to get into a rhythm. Then stride it out looking up, not at the pole. With a little practice and concentration you will find that walking four yards (12ft, 3.65m, or one horse stride) becomes very natural. If you ride a pony, practise walking four strides to 10ft (3m), or one pony stride.

   Now build two fences 72ft (21.9m) apart for horses, 60ft (18m) for ponies. Stand with your back to the first fence, in the centre of the fence with your heel at the base of it. Looking directly at the fence in front of you, take two strides. This will put you exactly on the spot where the horse should land over fence one. Then take four strides (i.e. one horse or pony stride), then another four, then another four, then another four and another four. It is vital while doing this not to look down at your feet. If you do, your strides will tend to become stilted. If your strides are the correct length, you will arrive exactly at the take-off point for the next fence, in other words two of your strides, or half a horse's stride, away.

The correct way to walk a related distance: from the centre of the first fence to the centre of the second.

Riding a related distance

Remember that it is the horse's stride pattern that is the key to riding related distances. This is why it is so important that you are in tune with what is happening underneath you, that your brain is in tune with what the horse's legs are doing. Only if you are in tune with your horse can you make the right decisions. Riding down related distances counting the strides aloud will help you to make the link between your brain and the horse's legs. Putting down poles between the fences will make him use himself, maintain balance and prevent rushing, in other words it will regulate his stride.

Related distance on a dog leg

This is a test which is seen more and more frequently as courses become increasingly technical. The designer will set two fences a few strides apart and slightly on an angle to each other. As a result he is making the rider determine the line to take from one to the other. This type of problem requires careful attention when you are walking the course. You must try to put yourself in the horse's position and think how he thinks. Stand with your back to the first fence and walk two paces to where the horse is going to land. Then look directly towards the next fence and start your turn almost immediately, on the first stride. The horse, having taken one stride, will be wondering whether the fence which has now come into his eyeline is the next one. After two strides he will be sure that it is. Even with a turn as short as this you can make it smooth and the horse will be totally aware of where he is required to go.

The mistake that so many riders make is to go straight on from the first fence and then make an acute turn to the second. Although the rider knows which fence he is aiming for, it won't even be in the horse's eyeline at this stage. Then, all of a sudden, the rider asks for a sharp turn, taking the horse by surprise. As a result he is bound to become unbalanced. You must remember that he needs to know where he is going and to maintain his rhythm.

If the dog-leg distance walks, say, four and a half strides, you must now make up your mind whether you are going to take four strides going a little forwards, or to opt for five shorter ones. This is where you need to be aware of the dog-leg rule: you will find that because of the turn, each of the horse's strides will automatically shorten by a small amount. Also, because the horse isn't quite sure to begin with where he is going next, he will hang back slightly off the bridle. This means that a dog-leg distance will actually ride a little longer than it walks and the four and a half strides will in reality ride more like four and three-quarters. Always remember this dog-leg rule when you walk the course and make your decisions accordingly. In the above instance you would normally be safer going for five strides.

There are various other factors to be taken into account when riding a dog-leg on a related distance. If the second fence is particularly flimsy there is no point in going on four strides – the risk factor would be too great. On the other hand, if this was a speed class, to be competitive you might need to ride it on four. In this case you would have to take a more direct line so as to take the curl out of the distance.

It all hinges on being able to walk the distance accurately, to assess the problem and to make the right decision for your horse in the particular circumstances. Always walk the line from centre to centre and then if necessary adjust it, either by going inside the line to take space out or outside it if you want more space.

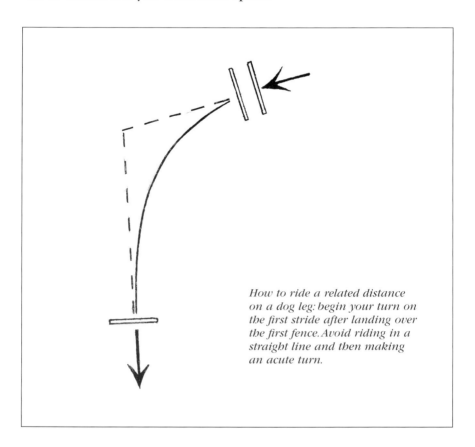

How to ride a related distance on a dog leg: begin your turn on the first stride after landing over the first fence. Avoid riding in a straight line and then making an acute turn.

Giving your horse gears

It is imperative for the show jumper to be able to shorten or lengthen his stride when requested. These downward and upward transitions can first be practised on the flat. To condense the canter, which will shorten the stride, close down with your hand, make a little gentle movement back with your body and keep your leg lightly on the horse. Don't put too much leg on, because then you will be sending him two different messages. Your leg will be saying go forward and your hand will be saying stop, which will confuse him. The important thing is not to allow him to break into trot. If he does, use a little more leg to move him back into canter immediately.

To practise shortening and lengthening the stride when jumping, build two fences on a five-stride distance, that is 72ft (21.9m) for a horse, 60ft (18m) for a pony. Ride it on six strides, which will mean that each canter stride must be 2ft (0.60m) shorter than normal for a horse, 18in (45cm) shorter for a pony. Then close down the canter even more so that the horse takes seven strides. Then lengthen the stride again by riding it on five. Remember when condensing the canter to close the contact, to be quite positive and to keep your body up – and don't use too much leg. The horse must be very soft to the fence. He should not attack it. Riders tend to override fences because they are a little nervous

A useful exercise for learning to ride on turns: four small jumps on a 30- or 40-metre circle.

and want to get the jump over and done with. What you must remember is that it is your job to get the horse to the take-off point; it is his job to jump the fences. When jumping a course keep concentrating on your horse's rhythm and stride pattern.

Once you and your horse can use the gears, you can start to ride on turns. An exercise I like to use is to build four small jumps – no more than 2ft 4in (70cm) high – on a 30- or 40-metre circle: fence, four strides, fence, four strides, fence, four strides, etc. Not only does this start to create and develop feel, it also makes the rider more aware of his body. Because on take-off you are already looking at the next fence, you learn to control your body, and your head position will be more correct. It also encourages you to think ahead. Too many riders make the mistake of jumping once fence and then having to regroup for the next and before they know it the next fence is upon them.

Riding without stirrups

Riding without stirrups helps you to develop balance and a much more secure position, though you should not attempt it until you are competent at jumping with stirrups and never without supervision. Practise over a couple of fences. Keep them small and only do a little at a time. Don't take your stirrups off the saddle, simply slip your feet from the irons. Losing your irons is something that sometimes happens in competition so this exercise can be very useful practice.

Getting left behind at the fence

Many riders through lack of confidence – possibly as the result of a bad fall – wait until the horse has taken off before they go into the jumping position. If you are still sitting in the saddle when the horse adjusts his balance backwards as he prepares for take off, you will suddenly find yourself getting left behind because he is going up and away from you. The only way to cure this fault is to start to be more positive in your body position. When you reach the jump, you must release the seat.

To encourage you to stay above the horse, build two or three little bounces. A bounce is quite an intricate movement, so if you try to sit to it you will be thrown all over the place. Practise over the bounces, being careful not to rush. If when you ride two or three bounces you get left behind, it means that your body balance is too much behind the horse's movement. If, on the other hand, you have to put your hands out to stop yourself going 'over the handlebars', your balance is in front of the horse. The only way to stay in balance over bounces is to adopt the jumping position and allow your knees to act as shock absorbers. That is what you should be thinking about at every single fence that you jump. Sitting and waiting until the horse has taken off is negative and tells the horse that you don't have faith in him. You cannot expect him to believe in you if you don't believe in yourself.

Horses who rush their fences

Horses are creatures of flight and don't normally attack things. If a horse does start attacking his fences, standing off a long way and landing a long way out, it means that he is not listening to his rider. The horse (and probably the rider as well) needs to be retrained. The answer is to use poles on the ground to regulate his stride. If he wants to rush, the poles will be in the wrong place for him. Use square poles, which are a little more defined than planks, to help create the required roundness of stride. The aim is to retrain by habit the way in which the horse goes.

Lay out four poles at 12ft (3.65m) intervals for a horse, 10ft (3m) for a pony, in front of a cross-pole fence and go down the line over and over again until the horse starts to concentrate on the approach. He will soon become more regular in his stride pattern. While riding over the poles it is very important to keep your body still. Jump these poles and the cross-pole each day for a week to get the horse into the habit of keeping his stride regular. Then you can gradually begin to reduce the number of poles.

To start with, remove the pole nearest to the fence. This means that the last stride is being left to the horse's own devices. When he can do this without rushing, remove the second pole, so that you are now only regulating the first two strides. Finally, remove the second to last pole, leaving three non-jumping strides from the one remaining pole to the fence. Ride over the remaining pole and the fence, calling the strides out loud as you go – 'one, two, three'. Don't make the mistake of includ-ing the landing over the first pole, only the three complete strides. Counting the strides in this way takes the emphasis off the jump and puts it more on the rhythm and the approach. The horse then begins to become softer and more relaxed.

Where many riders go wrong is that they are so busy looking for the fence that they will accept any type of approach as long as they clear it. What you must remember is: the better the approach, the more chance the horse has of jumping clear.

Coping with fillers

Many people find that when they first start competing their horses are spooked by fillers. It is usually a lack of confidence rather than naughtiness, but if you make an issue out of it, it can become a problem. If you have a young horse, or one who dislikes jumping fences with fillers, introduce some to your fences at home. If you don't have a full set of show jumps of your own, see if you can hire the arena the day after a show and practise over the fences there, keeping them very small to begin with in order to gain your horse's confidence.

Start by placing the fillers to the sides of the fence. Each time your horse has jumped the fence, ease the fillers in slightly. If you do this gradually, before he realises it he will be popping over the fence with the fillers in place. It is a good idea to use tubs of flowers – they move a little and challenge the horse optically. In no time at all your horse will be jumping a strange-looking fence confidently and bravely. Remember that the more you work with your horse the more confident he will become The more you try to force him, the more likely he is to resist you.

Examples of fillers that you might meet in a competition. The more you can practise at home over unusual fillers, the less likely they are to take your horse or pony by surprise at a show.

Above, below and opposite: different types of fillers that challenge a horse optically.

69

A filler which has vertical lines is more difficult for a horse than a plain one.

Difficulties riding shorter distances

The main reason that so many riders have problems when riding shorter distances is that they accelerate when approaching their fences. Under normal circumstances they don't realise that they are doing it. But when they come to ride a short distance, having too forward a jump will actually make the distance shorter. If you override going in to, say, a soft four strides, you will see how much harder the horse has to work to try to make the distance. He loses his shape and you will begin to wrestle with him. You will still be fighting with him on the last stride. Never forget that if you see a long stride to a fence, the chances are that there is a nice short stride directly behind it. You must be disciplined, you must tell your horse what you want him to do. If he finds shorter distances difficult, it isn't that he's not listening to you, it's more likely that you're telling him the wrong things.

Difficulties with half strides

Usually the problem here is that the rider changes his mind half way through. He intends to go, say, on five strides, but the horse lands over the first fence, takes a bit of a run and the rider suddenly decides to kick on and do the distance in four. One minute he is telling the horse 'we're waiting, we're waiting', the next he is giving him a big kick and sending him forward. This shows that the rider is neither disciplined nor convinced of his own actions. By changing your mind in such a

70

situation you run the risk of the horse not listening to you in future. You must stick to your guns. If you follow through your instructions, at least the horse will know what to expect. When you are training your horse, you need to have a clear idea of what you are trying to produce, and a distinct and definite way of producing it.

The worst scenario with half-stride distances is that the horse may have the fence down. He might even stop. But if you stick to your guns, you are at least being consistent rather than telling your horse that as you don't really know what you are doing you are going to panic. If you do that, the inevitable result will be that your horse will stop listening to you. Such indecisiveness will wreck your confidence and his.

Dealing with difficult combinations

A combination often seen in young rider classes or at national level finals involves one non-jumping stride between parts A (a vertical) and B (a spread) and one and three-quarter strides between parts B and C (another vertical). It is a very simple problem but one that is often wrongly executed.

The mistake is to approach in a soft, waiting fashion. This results in the horse landing a little short over part A and not going forward sufficiently. As a result you will be too far off the middle part and will have to give the horse a kick in order to throw him over the spread. In other words, you will have to press the forward button. However, when you do that you will then be going forward into a short distance. As a result, that distance – which is already short – will become shorter still.

The correct way to ride this type of combination is to come in fairly strongly – not galloping but quite forward. The horse then takes a proper full stride after jumping the first part and is able to back up in order to jump the second. As a result, the distance to the third part does not become shorter.

How to speed up your jump-off

Remember that in a jump-off it is the shortest, most economical route that usually wins. Fewer strides equal a faster round. By all means be speedy and economical within your chosen route, but remember that you must maintain balance and present the horse well enough at each fence for him to clear it. If you gallop round becoming longer and longer in your stride pattern, the chances are that he will have one or more fences down.

The turn-back, from one fence to another, is a movement often used by course designers in a jump-off. It requires practice, as you almost need to perform a turn on the haunches.

The way you execute turns in a jump-off against the clock can mean the difference between success and failure. When jumping at speed it is essential to keep the horse balanced and bending around your leg, with his hocks engaged; only then will he have the power to jump the fences. One way to improve your jump-off turns is by working round small fences or raised poles. Place four in a line and ride round them one at a time in a tight circle, steadily progressing up the line. Then change the rein and do the same thing on the other side. The horse's stride pattern should be very short and he should keep himself engaged and coming through from behind.

Another very different type of turn which course designers often use in a jump-off is the turn-back. This is when you have to jump one fence and then turn back and go in the opposite direction for the next. It is a difficult movement for the rider to stay in balance. To do it well you almost need to perform a turn on the haunches. Practise this by keeping a contact in the outside hand, a little rein pressure, and keeping the horse's neck straight so that he more or less falls through his shoulder and then immediately goes forwards. Practise on both reins.

You can often save valuable time against the clock by taking one or more fences at an angle.

Jumping at an angle

You can save time by jumping a fence at an angle but you must let the horse know very early on exactly where he is going and then maintain contact in both hands. Don't try to pull him in to the fence or he might simply run to one side. Funnel him in both hands and keep a good direct approach, event though it's on the angle.

5
All About Fences

In the early days of show jumping the fences used were simple hurdles, barriers and gates. Over the years it became important to introduce some variation into the obstacles, and gradually the design of both fences and courses has become more and more complex. The job of the course designer is to create problems to which the rider has to find solutions. He can't keep making the fences bigger and bigger but he can use different designs of fences and various little tricks to challenge both rider and horse. The more you understand what he is trying to do, the better you will be able to ride the course.

There are two basic types of fence: the vertical and the spread. A vertical or upright fence is one in which all the elements are in the same vertical plane, for example a set of poles one above the other.

Opposite *A wall is simply a type of vertical fence though this one is made more difficult for the horse to assess because of the viaduct arches painted on it.*

Top *In an ascending parallel the front rail is slightly lower than the back rail.*

Above *In a triple bar the second and third elements are higher than the one in front.*

As well as poles a vertical can be a wall, a gate, a set of planks or a combination of these. Spread fences include oxers (a slightly old-fashioned term for parallels), ascending parallels and Liverpools. A true parallel is a fence in which the front and back elements are exactly the same height. In an ascending parallel the front rail is slightly lower. Another type of ascending spread is the triple bar where the second and third elements are higher than the one in front. A Liverpool has a very low front rail, a water-tray and then a high rail. Even though it looks predominantly vertical, the front rail and water-tray actually create a spread fence.

When you see a fence that looks very wide and scary, remember the dimensions of a horse's stride. A 3ft-wide (0.915m) fence is only equivalent to a quarter of a stride. Express that in human terms, and it is the equivalent of a 9in (22.5cm) puddle. This puts into context just how much effort is required on the part of the horse and should make you feel more positive, because you will realise that such a fence is quite easy for the horse. Always study the problem that the course designer has provided – perhaps a double of spreads or a double of verticals – and try to turn it into a positive. You mustn't let the course designer intimidate you and cause you to make a mistake by over-riding a fence or transferring your nervousness down into your horse.

Groundlines

It is important to remember that the horse judges a fence from its base, so the groundline is a very important aspect of training the show jumper. Always keep the groundline in the same vertical plane as the fence or, to give a horse confidence and when training younger horses, bring it out anything up to 16 or 20 inches (40 or 50cm) in front of the vertical plane. This will encourage the horse to make a better shape through his shoulder. Be careful not to jump too many fences either without a groundline at all or with a false groundline (i.e. one that is beyond the vertical plane of the fence). The horse will be unable to judge exactly where the fence is and his confidence will be seriously undermined.

Modern show jumping calls for a very careful horse because fences are being built with much lighter materials and shallower cups than of old. Colours used to be very bold too – either red and white, black and white or blue and white. Nowadays course designers often use pastel shades, which are more difficult for horses to judge: they don't see the full spectrum of colours and although they are very good at picking out

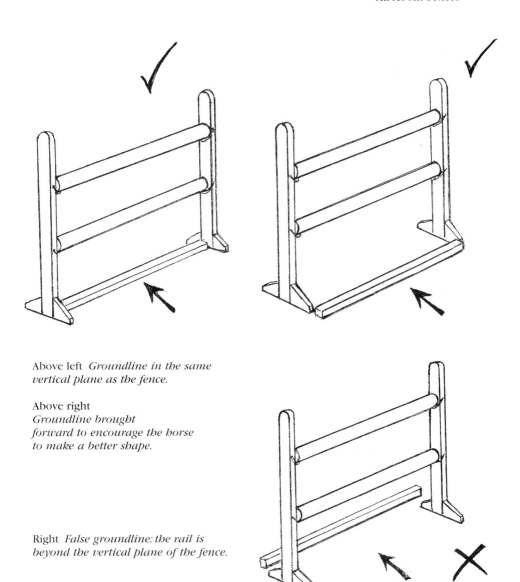

Above left *Groundline in the same vertical plane as the fence.*

Above right *Groundline brought forward to encourage the horse to make a better shape.*

Right *False groundline: the rail is beyond the vertical plane of the fence.*

contrast, a fence that is all white or all black, for instance, is more diffi-cult for them to see and invariably doesn't jump well. It is also becom-ing more and more usual, certainly at international shows, to site a fence in line with something that either blends in with it or sticks out like a sore thumb. The blending-in problem – for example a set of white rails in front of white boards round the edge of the arena – is a particularly tricky one because the lack of definition makes it difficult for the horse to judge.

Difficult fillers

There are a number of different types of filler which can be used to test you and your horse. White, for instance, is quite difficult for a horse to pick up. Also, a filler which has vertical lines or one that is not completely solid will pose problems. A wall, on the other hand, helps the horse because it has a solid groundline and is easier for him to size up.

When riding a fence with an unusual filler the golden rule is not to be tempted to attack it. The more you push your horse into something he is not sure of, the more he will back off and ignore your leg. By pushing him, you are asking him to stand off and be brave when he is clearly unsure. If you do that, you will end up being too far off the fence at take-off. Instead of attacking, you must keep the horse between your hand and leg – in other words keep the contact through the reins and keep your legs around him; it will give him confidence to know that you are not panicking. If you see a really long stride at this type of fence, simply keep cool and wait for the next, short stride. If you panic or are indecisive, the horse will feel it at once. Keep the contact between your hand and leg and the chances are that although he may be more wary of this type of fence and jump it extra carefully, he won't stop.

Swedish oxer or St Andrew's Cross

The idea behind this kind of fence, with its two sets of opposite slant-ing poles, is to challenge the horse by creating an optical illusion. To grasp the problem that it poses we need to understand how the horse sees. Because his eyes are set on the sides of his head, he has a nearly

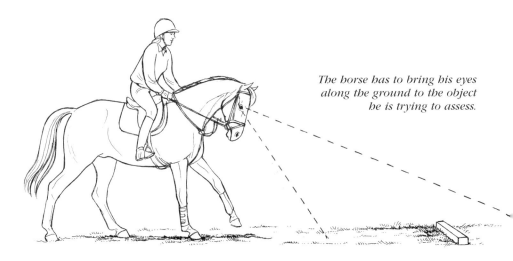

The horse has to bring his eyes along the ground to the object he is trying to assess.

all-round angle of vision. This enables him to see anything which might be going to attack him (and originally, of course, helped him to survive in the wild). When we come to teach a horse to jump, the disadvantage of this type of vision is that he finds it more difficult than we do, with our forward-facing eyes, to focus on a particular object directly in front of him. He has to lower his head and neck and bring his eyes along the ground to the object he is trying to assess: so something that is parallel to the ground is easier for him to judge than something that is slanting. The Swedish oxer can be made even more difficult if the course design-er introduces a filler between the two sets of slanting rails. Because it will be slightly behind the front line of the fence the horse will have no true groundline to help him judge the obstacle.

The optical illusion effect of a Swedish oxer makes it twice as difficult for a horse to jump as a normal fence whose components are parallel to the ground. It may stand only 1.25m high, but it is a great deal more difficult to jump than a normal 1.25m oxer. A course designer will often introduce this type of problem in a class where there is a big entry and where he has to find some way of achieving a result despite having to keep the fences within a certain height limit.

The big temptation for the rider is to approach the fence not in the middle but to the side where the front set of rails is lowest. However, because the far rails slant the other way the horse might think that you are aiming him at the high side. To avoid confusing him in this way, you should always keep to the central line. Ride the direct line and you'll find that, as long as he has confidence in you, your horse will accept the optical illusion with no problem. It is when you come to ride this type of fence that you will appreciate the importance during your initial training of keeping your horse straight. If he habitually tends to jump to one side, one day you will come upon a Swedish oxer that is built the wrong side for you and you may find yourself in difficulties.

Viaduct wall

This type of fence, with a rail or rails over a wall with 'arches' may look straightforward, but again because of the way the horse sees, it is inclined to cause problems. A plain wall, without the holes, is far easier to jump than a fence with a broken groundline, which makes the horse deeply suspicious. Course designers use it to put pressure on you, the rider. As with the Swedish oxer, the answer is not to panic. Keep the contact and keep your leg around the horse.

The broken groundline of the viaduct wall filler makes this fence more difficult for the horse to weigh up.

Planks

Most riders hate having to jump a set of planks, the main reason being that planks, unlike poles, are normally set on very flat cups so that if the horse so much as puts a toe on the top one it will slide straight off. Horses don't know that, of course. To a horse, planks look solid. They are also usually painted in sharp, easily distinguishable colours so they are in fact very horse-friendly. The problem here is definitely a rider one. Because riders know that this is a very delicate fence they tend to come in with much more pressure than to other fences, almost saying to their horses 'don't touch these, they'll come off too easily'. In other words, they panic and cause their horses to make mistakes.

Planks require a good technique on the part of the horse. Your hands must be very soft. Don't be too abrupt. If you try to snatch the horse off the ground, the chances are that either his head will go up and his front legs will dangle, or he will take out the planks behind. The solution is to ride at the fence in the opposite way, daring the horse a little. Often the horses who jump planks the best are the ones who are left alone by their riders.

A set of planks is a horse-friendly fence but riders tend to override them because they know that the cups are flat and the top plank is easily dislodged.

Liverpool or water ditch

Rails over a water ditch cause a great many problems, again because the horse is suspicious of the broken groundline. Any ditch, whether it is permanent or simply a portable water tray, interrupts his focus and makes him suspicious. The solution is to ride with plenty of panache into your hands. What you mustn't do is to ride forward and then suddenly drop your hands, so that the horse ends up leaning down into the fence and stopping, or sliding into it. You must use a solid hand contact, almost as if you are holding a child's hand and saying 'Come on, it's okay, it won't hurt you'. Use plenty of leg, but don't go for a long distance. You cannot get too deep to this fence. If you go on a long stride, the chances are that the horse just won't pick up from it.

A word of warning: it is crucial for you not to attempt to jump this type of fence on a young horse who has not had plenty of preparation. Build a little Liverpool at home and practise over it to give your horse confidence. You don't need a full-size water tray for the ditch – you can use a narrow strip of blue carpet or even a piece of blue tarpaulin from a DIY shop, as long as you make sure that the edges are weighted down and will not blow up in the wind while the horse is jumping. Training is definitely the key here. On a horse who has been correctly prepared and is confident, this type of fence should not cause a problem.

You can easily construct a Liverpool to practise over using blue carpet or a sheet of tarpaulin in place of a water ditch.

Water jump

The water jump poses a big headache for many riders and, unfortunately, for many horses too. The course designer's aim is to try to break the rhythm of both rider and horse: to jump water successfully you have to lengthen the stride and then have the discipline and control to shorten it again. Often the course designer will use a water jump in conjunction with another fence. He may put a fence on a short distance going to the water, or a flimsy vertical on a related distance after it. In both cases the aim is to test your ability to lengthen or shorten your horse's stride.

Most water jumps are between 12ft (3.65m) and, at championship level, 16ft (3.66m), wide. It sounds quite big and at championship level it is, but put in context with the horse's stride, even at 16ft it is only the equivalent of a stride and a quarter. Bearing in mind that the horse can take off much closer to this fence than usual because it is not very high, and that he may land, say, 6 to 10 inches (15 to 25cm) beyond the tape on the far side, he is still actually only having to take about a stride and a third. In human terms that is the equivalent of about 4½ft (1.37m) so it is not nearly as bad as it might at first appear.

The secret to jumping water successfully is to have the horse going on a long, forward-type of canter – not a flat-out gallop, with the reins flapping at him, which will merely make him panic. Try to get into a good cog, a good solid, forward-going canter with a good rhythm. By doing that and keeping the contact to give the horse confidence, you should be able to ride 'off the boards', that is as close as possible to the little take-off fence. The closer you are there, the less effort the horse has to make to reach the other side. If your canter is too forward and too flat, the chances are that you will not be as accurate in your take-off position. There is no point in having a really long canter if you end up taking off a long way from the water.

During training it is a good idea to place poles over the water jump in order to encourage the horse to achieve height. It is the same technique as that used by a human long jumper; the first thing he does when he hits the board is to try to gain height. Combined with speed, this gives you length as well. By teaching the horse to gain height as well as jumping the spread, when you come to jump water in a competition he should land in balance, not on his forehand. Therefore, if the course designer has used a fence on a related distance after the water, it won't cause you problems.

For training purposes a water jump does not have to be very wide. Placing a rail over the water teaches a horse to gain height and therefore to land in better balance.

If you have a young horse, don't wait too long before you start training him to jump water. Use a portable tray with boards in front of it. It does not need to be very wide. If a horse can pop happily over a 4-5ft (1.22-1.52m) water on a regular basis, he will have the confidence to take on bigger waters when he is seven or eight years old.

Natural gradients

Where natural gradients occur in an arena, the course designer is sure to make good use of them to try to stop you jumping a clear round. The key here is to remember that the horse uses the ground for focusing. As he comes downhill, his eye will be following the contour of the ground. As a result a fence set on a downhill gradient will draw him in deep because the ground is running away from him. If a fence is set on an uphill gradient, where the ground is coming up to meet him, he will tend to stand off it. The rule of thumb therefore is that going downhill pulls you into the bottom of a fence, going uphill puts you further off the fence.

This is an occasion when you must adjust your pace. You need to ride to an uphill fence with a little more strength to your canter. Be aware, though, that this does not mean more speed and certainly not too much length – just a little more panache. Coming downhill, you must soften your approach and give the horse time to use himself.

6

Going to Shows

There is a lot to think about when you start competing, so it makes sense to do as much forward planning as you can. If you are competing under Pony Club or BSJA rules, be sure to study the rule books, taking particular note of what items of dress you may or may not use and which items of tack are permitted. It may sound obvious, but do make absolutely sure that you know exactly where the show is, and plan your route in advance, allowing plenty of time for the journey. There is nothing worse than arriving at a show at the last minute and then having to rush.

Dress

You don't have to spend a fortune on clothes but you should always aim to look neat and tidy when you are competing. Make sure that all your riding things are clean and pressed and your boots polished at least the day before the show. See the Pony Club publication ***Correct Dress for Riders.***

Protective headgear is mandatory whether you are riding at a Pony Club show or under BSJA rules and must be manufactured to one of the minimum standards listed in the appropriate rule book. All hats or helmets must be worn with the chinstrap correctly and securely fastened. Hats or helmets that require covers should be worn with a plain, dark-coloured peaked cover.

You can wear either jodhpurs with jodhpur boots, or breeches with long boots. Jodhpurs and breeches should be white, pale yellow or fawn – dark colours are not permitted. In Pony Club competitions (but not in BSJA affiliated classes) you can instead wear plain black or brown half-chaps with standard riding or jodhpur boots of the same colour.

Unless the weather is very hot and the judges permit competitors to ride without one, you should always wear a jacket when in the arena.

It can be either tweed, dark navy or black. Underneath you should wear a white or pastel-coloured shirt with a tie. Pony Club members may wear a Pony Club tie with a tweed jacket, or a Pony Club tie or a white hunting stock with a navy blue or black jacket. Under BSJA rules you may, if you wish, wear a coloured tie or stock with a tweed jacket. Always secure your tie or stock with a tie-pin, and for safety wear it horizontally or at an angle, not vertically. Women are allowed to wear a specially designed show jumping shirt, again in white or pastel shades, fitted with a high white collar and no tie. Gloves and body protectors are optional. Junior riders may wear a body protector either under or over their jackets. For adults, the body protector should be under the jacket.

A whip is permitted under both Pony Club and BSJA rules but it must be no longer than 75cm and no shorter than 45cm overall. Be aware that in Pony Club competitions a rider who hits her horse or pony before the start of the course may, at the judges' discretion, be eliminated. Spurs are also permitted, though again there are strict rules governing their dimensions; under Pony Club rules they must be blunt, without rowels or sharp edges, and must not exceed 3cm in length. Unless you hold the Pony Club B Test, you must have written permission from your District Commissioner if you wish to wear spurs. Under BSJA rules, again the length is restricted to 3cm and although rowels are allowed, their diameter must not be in excess of 1cm. In BSJA pony classes, only blunt spurs with necks not exceeding 2cm are allowed.

Getting ready

So that you don't forget anything, make a check-list of all the things you could need at the show and then go through this the night before to make sure that you have everything cleaned and prepared. Items to include on your check-list are:

For the horse
For travelling:
- Headcollar and lead rope
- Spare headcollar and lead rope
- Leg bandages/padding
- Tail bandage/tail guard
- Rugs/roller

At the show
- Grooming kit
- Studs and tool for fitting
- Equine first-aid kit
- Canister of fresh water (water is not always as readily available at showgrounds as it should be)
- Water bucket
- Feed/haynet
- Emergency repair kit

For the rider:
- Shirt
- Tie or stock
- Tie-pin
- Breeches or jodhpurs
- Boots
- Jacket
- Hat with chin harness
- Hairnet, if you have long hair
- Gloves
- Whip
- Spurs, if worn
- Waterproof coat in case of bad weather
- First-aid kit

In your emergency repair kit include items such as safety pins, needle and thread, black insulation tape, a hole punch and some elastic bands. Put everything in a bag which your helper can take to the collecting ring. If anything goes wrong at the last minute, the chances are that you will be able to fix it.

When loading your trailer or lorry make sure that everything on the check-list is on board.

Travelling

If you have never travelled your horse or pony before, it is as well to have a little practice at loading and unloading and taking him on the odd short journey before the day of your first show. Even if you have been assured by his previous owner that he is a good traveller – and most horses and ponies do travel happily in today's trailers and boxes –

it is best to be absolutely sure. The last thing you want is a panic on the morning of your first competition. If your horse does become restive when travelling, try one or two experiments. Some horses prefer to face backwards rather than forwards and some will travel better if they have more room to spread their feet to balance themselves. If a horse finds his stall too narrow he might end up leaning on the partition in order to keep his balance and may then slip which will result in him panicking. Removing the partition to give him more space usually solves this problem.

If you have a horse who is reluctant to load there are various ways of encouraging him. Parking the trailer or horsebox against a wall or other barrier will make it impossible for him to duck out on that side. It is natural for a horse to be suspicious of an unfamiliar vehicle, so make sure that the inside light is on and if there is a front unloading ramp, open this and lead the horse through a few times to familiarise him with the

The horse dressed for travelling. For short distances, protect his legs with leg-wraps. For longer journeys he should wear bandages.

vehicle. If necessary, tempt him in with a little food or lead another horse in first and let him follow to give him confidence. A horse who is reluctant to go up a steep ramp may load perfectly well if you park the vehicle so that the ramp is on raised ground and the angle less steep. The golden rule is to be patient and keep calm. If you become cross, the horse will simply be more scared and difficult.

Your vehicle must be serviced regularly to avoid the possibility of breaking down – a nightmare when you are transporting horses. It should also be cleaned out after every journey and the floor should be checked regularly. If the box has rubber matting turn this back to make sure that the boards are in sound condition; floorboards can rot and cause serious accidents. Make sure that the box is clean and ready to go the day before your show.

If the journey time to the show is less than an hour, fit your horse with leg-wraps that fasten with Velcro. For longer journeys it is better to use bandages but you must be very careful to use adequate padding underneath and to fit them just tightly enough to prevent them from slipping, but not so tightly that they interfere with the horse's circulation. Bandaging is quite an art, so get an experienced person to show you how.

At the show

If you have planned your journey carefully, you will have plenty of time when you arrive at the showground to park, locate the secretary's office (where you will collect your number), the loos (most important!) and familiarise yourself with the layout of the collecting ring and the arenas. Check all the facilities so that you are not rushing about at the last minute wondering where to go.

Find out exactly where your ring is and what competition is going on. A lot of show jumping competitions run on one after another and shows don't give you a specific start time, so it is important to find out which class is on, how may riders there are and then spend a minute or two working out when your class is likely to begin. Ask what method is being used for going in to jump: do you just put your number on the number board, or is there a drawn order? Look at the ground conditions. Is the going in the ring hard? Are horses slipping? What sort of studs are they wearing? Ask someone or watch a few horses as they come out. You can learn a lot by watching and talking to other people.

It might be a good idea to take your horse off the lorry well before

Having friends or family to lend a hand at a show is a great help.

your class and let him have a look round so that you can judge his reactions. If he is excited or nervous, walking him about for a while may help to relax him before you start to work. You must avoid rushing. If you don't give yourself and your horse enough time to prepare correctly you will probably make a mess of things and will end up losing confidence.

Warming up

Because every horse is different it is impossible to lay down hard and fast rules about how much warming up you should do. It is a question of learning from experience. A horse who jumps off adrenalin and is better when he's a little fresh may just need loosening up for five minutes before he starts jumping because you want to keep that explosive energy. On the other hand, a horse with too much sharp energy may need taking to a quiet corner for around 25 minutes for some very soft work to release the tension. With some horses, the more work

Start your jumping warm-up over a small cross-pole fence. Remember to call out 'cross-pole' as you approach it to tell other riders where you are heading.

Don't over-do the jumping before you compete. One bigger fence just before you go into the arena is usually sufficient to ensure that the horse has his eye in.

you do the more tense they become. If you find that your horse doesn't get any better through being worked, the next time you go to a show simply give him less. It is a question of learning to know your horse and the best way of preparing him and then getting into a routine. You may do something for the right reason and find it doesn't have the desired effect, so try a different way next time. It's all part of being a horse person.

If the arena is a normal size, you will probably need to start doing a little warm-up jumping when there are about ten to twelve riders still to go before you. Indoors, where things happen a bit faster, it could be from twelve to fifteen: at a very large arena, such as Hickstead, where horses take much longer to go round, you would only need to allow around six to eight. Start your jumping warm-up with a very small fence, probably a cross-pole, and pop your horse over a couple of times on either rein. Then gradually build the fence up, asking him to land on the left lead, then on the right, feeling how he reacts. Make sure that he lands softly and not running, that he is polite and listening to you and not too excitable. All the time you should be trying to get him to relax between his jumps. Then build a small oxer. As a general rule it is best not to jump very big fences before a competition. In fact, under Pony Club rules it is not permitted to jump practice fences that are higher or wider than the maximum dimensions of the fences in the competition. Perhaps just the last jump before you go into the ring might be a vertical at the same height as the fences in the arena – something just to make sure that the horse has his eye in. Remember that this is a warm-up. Don't try to run the race before you've done the race. Some people take their horses into the ring puffing and tired, overheated and overdone. This is a big mistake. The aim is to time your warm-up so that when you go into the ring you get the best out of your horse. He should be relaxed, comfortable, confident and ready to go and do his best.

When warming up, always be aware of where everybody else is in the collecting ring. Remember that the rule is to pass left to left – though just because you know this it doesn't mean that everyone else does. It is also good manners to tell other people which fence you are planning to jump. Get into the habit of calling out 'vertical' or 'oxer' when approaching a practice fence. Never ride too close to the horse in front. Be aware of other people doing the same to you and if necessary ask, politely, for more room, explaining if appropriate that you have a young or nervous horse. Remember that you are all fellow competitors and others might be just as nervous as you.

Walking the course

Always make the most of the opportunity to walk the course. Give yourself plenty of time and don't waste it gossiping with friends. It requires 100 per cent concentration. If you are not very experienced, find someone more knowledgeable to walk with so that you can ask for their advice. Always try to walk the basic line that you are planning to ride rather than darting across from one fence to the next. By walking your exact line you may pick up certain points that might not be apparent if you simply cut from one fence to another. For instance there might be a white vehicle parked outside the arena but positioned directly behind one of the jumps and it might look as if the two are much closer together than they really are. This could be a potential source of confusion for your horse, so you should be aware of it before-hand. If you were to walk a different line you might not see that. Keep a nice central position to each fence, walk the distance from one fence to the next and work out your strides. Use the words forwards and backwards when thinking about strides. If you think 'forward' you will land over a fence and then just gently ease the stride forward to the next.

Correctly turned-out Pony Club members walking the course at their Show Jumping Championships. Always give yourself plenty of time for the course walk and give it 100% concentration.

Remember the rule when measuring related distances: walk centre to centre from one fence to the next.

Opposite *Clearing this fence in good style - and already looking for the next.*

If there is time, watch the first few riders jump the course to see how the different fences ride.

Bear in mind that jumping into a corner will tend to stifle the horse's approach, so you must be sure that he takes a central line and doesn't jump across the fence; a lot of horses do that when they anticipate a turn immediately afterwards. Always use the full corners of the arena.

Making sharp turns is likely to shorten the horse's stride, whereas getting him into the habit of using the full arena helps maintain rhythm and balance. Keep your turns smooth, so that they accommodate your stride pattern. The more the stride suffers, the more chance there is that the jump will suffer.

By walking the course correctly and assessing the problems before-hand, you will be able to devise a plan. That is not to say that things will always go according to plan, but if you have a target to aim for you can be decisive. Horses can't walk the course, but they do know if you are nervous, frightened or indecisive. By getting into the habit of walking the course correctly you will become more accurate in your riding and as a result the horse will improve. If you try to go round and just jump the fences willy-nilly, the chances are that you will make a lot of mistakes and the horse will stop listening to you.

As you leave the ring, go through the course in numerical order as quickly as you can, pointing at each fence in turn. Don't leave the arena until you have it fixed in your mind. Remembering courses is all part of the learning process. You must devise a system that works for you and be able to block everything out. Make sure, too, that you know where the judges are situated.

If there is time before you are due in the arena, stand and watch the first few riders jumping the course until it is time for you to get mounted. This will give you an opportunity to see how particular fences are riding.

Riding the course

Be prepared to enter the ring a little early: preferably as the previous person is jumping the last fence. This means that as they're finishing their round you can be having a little canter round; you'll gain 10, 15 or 20 seconds, and although it doesn't sound a lot it's actually quite a long time for you and your horse to have a look round the arena. If there is a particularly spooky part of the course, ride around that part and let your horse have a look at it. You have 45 seconds from when the bell rings to when you have to start your round and that gives you plenty of time to check on things such as whether the planks and the gate are correctly positioned on the cups. If you see something about a fence that doesn't look right, stand by the fence and raise your hand to the judges. They will stop the clock and check it out.

When riding a course always think about canter, rhythm, line. Make a smooth turn into the first fence and allow the horse to see where he is going. Remember that the horse hasn't walked the course. When coming to the first fence it is very important that you quickly tell him which fence you want him to jump – bearing in mind that it might not be the first fence he sees. Make sure that he is focusing on the correct fence straight away. It might be that there is another fence beyond the first one, but as long as you keep a good central line of approach that should not affect the way he jumps. Use the full turns and look at the next fence nice and early.

Remember that some fences are more difficult for a horse. White, for example, is often used by course designers because it tends to cause problems: the lack of contrast makes it more difficult for the horse to focus. You must not lose your cool, even if your horse spooks. You will need to keep him on an elastic contact, to close your leg around him to reassure him. The chances are that even if he does take a look at a spooky fence, he will nevertheless jump it. In such a situation don't panic. The horse is looking to you for reassurance so it is vital to keep cool and think positive. If he were to back off the fence a little and you were to panic, you might well make him stop.

If your horse has a fence down, don't let it distract you. Forget about it and concentrate on the next one. Remember to go through the finish,

Remember to keep riding until you're through the finish!

97

and don't leave the arena directly after jumping the last fence. Get your horse back in control and walking on a soft rein. Give him a pat, even if you have had a bad round. Remember that while you're in the ring you are in the showcase, in the eye view of everybody, so don't resort to tantrums just because things have not gone well.

Retiring before completing your round

Remember that retiring before you have completed your round is not a shameful thing. It is not necessarily the same as giving up: in fact it can very often be a positive move. If, for example, your horse has a problem at a particular fence and becomes unsettled you may simply make the problem worse by persevering. There is always another day. Watch the top riders and you will see that they are much more likely to retire than the average amateur. If things are not going well – perhaps they have made a mistake and are out of the reckoning or maybe the ground is not as good as they had hoped – they would prefer to save the horse for another day.

If for whatever reason you do decide to retire before completing your round, you should indicate your intentions to the judge by stopping and raising your hand.

Jump-offs

If you jump a clear round study the jump-off course and plot your route as soon as possible. You can't walk the jump-off course so it is really important to study it, memorise the order of the fences and work out your route. Sometimes you may find there are two or three fences that were not in round one, so you will need to locate them. Riders tend to have their own system for remembering jump-off courses. I like to think of the fences as one, two, three, four, five, etc, even though they may technically be numbered one, four, seven, nine, 11ab, 13, etc. The important thing is to choose a system that works for you so that you aren't confused when you go into the ring.

When planning your track look out for the simple turn. Sometimes you can save two or three strides by turning inside a fence rather than going round it. But remember that although taking fewer strides invariably means that you are quicker, you can only go as fast as you can jump clear. It is particularly important when planning a jump-off that you know exactly what your horse is capable of. If, for instance, he negotiates turns better on one rein than the other you might be better to avoid a sharp turn on his less good side. If you find that he tends to become careless when he goes quickly you would do better to aim for classes where speed is not so essential.

As well as knowing your horse's capabilities, you should also be aware of the competition. If you are followed in the jump-off by some-one whose horse is not particularly fast, there is no point in trying to set a speed record and risk having a fence down, thereby handing them the class on a plate. Learn to work things out, play the game and set a target that is realistic for your horse. Use your brain and never expect him to do the impossible. Bear in mind that you won't always win, even over a course that suits you, so you are even less likely to win over one that doesn't.

Feeding and watering on competition days

If you plan to compete regularly it is a good idea to devise a feeding programme that you can follow whether your horse is at home or at a show. Horses love routine so if they are normally given a substantial feed at lunchtime they will naturally expect to have the same when they are away competing. Not receiving it will add to the stress of going to shows. My horses are fed as normal on the morning of a show day, at least an hour and a half before they travel. But because they are only given a scoop of nuts for lunch at home they don't expect a large lunch when they are competing.

Feeding and watering competition horses is a matter of common sense. Make sure that you have fresh water available but only allow your horse regular little sips. Wringing out a clean sponge in his mouth will also help to relieve dryness. Remember that on show days horses tend not to pass droppings as regularly as when they are at home and most won't stale while they are on the lorry. Being grazing animals, they are designed to be constantly on the move and it cannot do them any good to stand for long periods 'holding on' to quantities of food and water. If you can it is a good idea to lead your horse out to a quiet corner of the showground and let him graze for a little while. It will encourage him to relax and he may well stale while he is there.

I never feed my horses on the lorry – not even hay (apart from anything else hayseeds tend to blow into their faces, especially then they travel herringbone). As a result I have never had a case of colic when travelling.

7

Putting it All into Practice

To give you an idea of the type of questions you will be asked in a typical competition – and how to come up with the correct answers with your particular horse – I have designed a course which I am going to walk with two imaginary riders, Tom and Sarah. Tom is on a 17hh Warmblood – quite a big-striding horse – and Sarah is on a 15.3hh three-quarter Thoroughbred.

The course walk

Let us imagine that it is a big show and the time schedule is quite tight. You have been allowed 15 minutes to walk the course. This may sound a long time but actually it isn't, so be ready to go into the arena as soon as the course is ready.

Begin by looking for **Fence 1**, which you will see is hidden behind a bank of flowers. It is a straightforward parallel oxer with a rustic fence and a brush filler. The only problem is that it is quite close to the end of the arena and near the entrance. To approach on the left rein would mean making a fairly sharp turn, so I am going to advise you both to come on the right rein, past the entrance, through the start and back on yourselves, as it were, to Number 1. This will give you a bigger, wider turn to the fence. Also, by slightly overshooting it you will have a better line to Number 2.

The problem to look out for with the approach to **No. 2** is that your horse might think you are aiming for No. 5 backwards. Picture it from the horse's point of view: when you come to No. 1 one you can see that No. 2 is to the left-hand side, but for a second or two it looks as if you are heading for the landing side of No. 5. To avoid confusing the horse you need to slightly overshoot No. 1, which means aiming more towards the judges' box, so that it becomes very apparent that you are

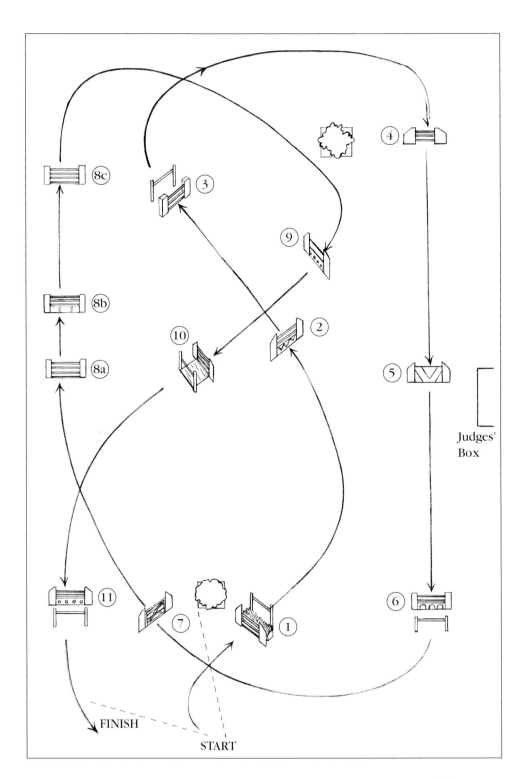

not going to jump No. 5 backwards but are in fact heading for No. 2 – a red and black vertical.

Fence 3, a red and white oxer (just poles, no fillers) is in a straight line from No. 2 but is on a related distance which you will need to walk. It walks 15⅓ yards, approximately 46ft (about 14m): roughly translated, that is 2¾ strides of the average horse. So this distance is a bit short for three strides – though I don't think anyone will try going down it on two. Because the distance is slightly short you must be careful not to over-ride Fence 2. Going into a soft, short distance you should not be too forward. If you see a long stride as you approach No. 2, remember that it is not going to do you any good. Wait a little longer and get a bit deeper: this will help you because you will decelerate, pop over 2 and then get a nice, even three strides to 3.

You must also take care here because you will be aiming directly at the grandstand and there will be a lot of movement in your horse's eye-line. You must make sure that he is concentrating on the fence and not being distracted by people moving about in the stand.

After jumping No. 3 you have to turn right-handed round the bank of flowers to **Fence 4**; course designers use the flowers not only to dress the arena but also to present you with an alternative route between fences. Sometimes you will want to go round them; on other occasions you might want to cut inside. In fact here there is no opportunity to go inside to No. 4.

Fence 4 is a very narrow stile, only 8ft (2.75m) wide. The blue and yellow poles are positioned directly one above the other so that the colours and lines match in. Note that the cups on this fence are quite delicate. The important thing to remember when jumping a stile is not to attack it. Horses tend to be wary of jumping narrow fences like this and, as a general rule, they don't stand off them. A word of warning in this situation: don't go on too committed a long stride because your horse will probably back off, put in an extra stride and end up making a mistake.

After the stile there is a straight line to **Fence 5** – a set of yellow and blue planks which are on flat cups, and then directly behind that an oxer. There are related distances between 4 and 5 and between 5 and 6. The distance between 4 and 5 walks exactly 22 yards, that is 66ft (20.1m), or in horse terms exactly 4½ strides. In this situation there is no 'yes' or 'no' answer – you must do what best suits your individual horse.

Tom, with his big-striding horse, should keep coming on four strides;

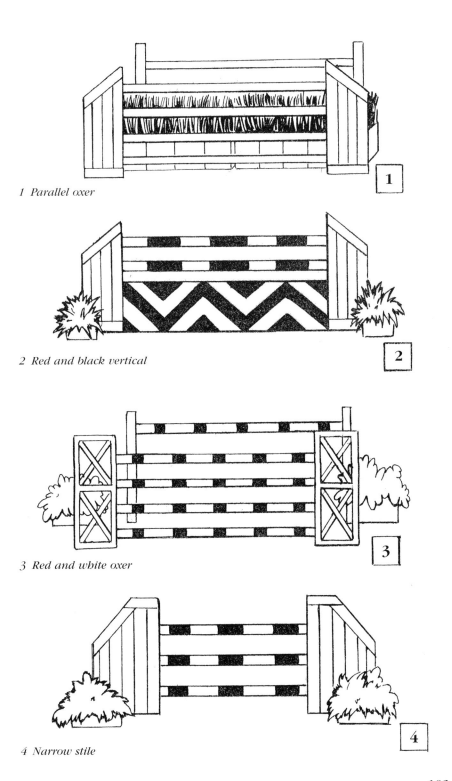

1 Parallel oxer

2 Red and black vertical

3 Red and white oxer

4 Narrow stile

to try to fit in five will disrupt the horse's rhythm and he might end up fighting Tom and having the planks down. Sarah, on the other hand, with her 'busy' horse, will do better to wait for the five strides; if she tries to go on four her horse may well become too flat.

Remember that at a set of planks the more you can get your horse to relax, the better he is going to jump them. Don't do what so many riders do – which is to ride with a lot more force, putting more pressure on the horse. If you do, he will probably not be in the correct shape and he only has to drop one little toe on the top plank to put you on four faults. Remember that planks are on flat cups and it takes only a slight tap for the top one to slide off.

The distance from Fence 5 to 6, a blue and white oxer with half-moon shaped viaduct walls underneath, is the same as between the two previous fences: 4½ strides. Apart from the related distance, the problem posed here is the broken groundline, which is designed to test the horse's trust in his rider; he is not going to be able to judge the fence as well as one with a solid groundline. A horse who doesn't trust his rider will automatically become more wary, but for a horse and rider who are working well together this fence should not cause too many problems.

Both riders should aim to do the second related distance on the same strides as the first: that is, Tom should go for four and Sarah for five. Both will thus keep in balance and avoid confusing their horses. As Tom lands over the stile he should be saying in his mind 'give a little squeeze' whereas Sarah should be saying 'just wait a little'.

After the oxer you must be very careful, because the entrance to the arena is directly in front of you and you have to make a sharp right-hand turn to **Fence 7**. The angle here is quite acute and if you are not on the ball as you land over No. 6 you may almost go past your line, miss your turn and find yourself having to re-organise. This is another course designer's trick.

As soon you have jumped No. 6 you must immediately look at Fence 7, so that your body and mind are already prepared for the turn. By doing that you will start to turn just that little bit earlier and should be in just the right place. Fence 7 is a gate, a fence which usually jumps well. Horses who have been hunting or done cross-country have a lot of respect for gates because they know that under normal circum-stances they don't knock down. In show jumping, of course, they are placed on flat cups so horses who lack this cross-country experience will soon realise that they only have to tap them for them to fall.

5

5 Yellow and blue planks

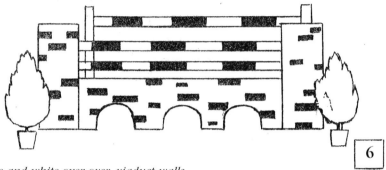

6

6 Blue and white oxer over viaduct walls

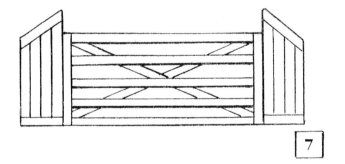

7

7 Gate

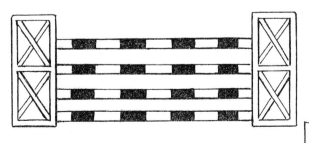

8 | a & c

8a & c Green and white verticals

Although this should be a straightforward fence, bear in mind that there is a flower bank close by which could well distract your horse, especially in windy conditions, when the flowers tend to sway about. The flowers are not there just for decoration!

After the gate comes the green and white combination: a vertical to an oxer to a vertical. This is a fair way from Fence 7 and there is no related distance. **8a to 8b** walks one stride but is approximately 1ft (30cm) too long. In other words it is not incredibly long but it is a little open or forward. **8b to 8c** walks two strides but is a little short – more like 1¾ strides. What the course designer is asking here is (1) can the rider judge the fact that the combination is first long, then short, and (2) can the horse go in forward but then back himself up so that he doesn't make up too much ground coming out?

The key to riding this type of combination is to jump in a little more forward than you would like. By doing this, your stride will be a little longer and will therefore match the distance. At 8b you will be hoping that your horse will prop and get a good round bascule and that he will land more steeply and a little flat-footed, which will enable him to shorten to come out. Here it is largely up to the horse to shorten himself: you can help him a little, but if you are not careful you may start to help too much with your hand. This may cause him to 'invert' his shape and he could well pull off the third element behind. My advice is to approach 8a with a nice strong rhythm; then, as you jump in, sit quietly, allowing your horse to back off 8b. As you land over 8b you should keep your body nicely up and in balance to allow your horse to shorten.

After the combination there is another quite wide turn to **Fence 9**, a set of white rails with a board filler. The two little problems to be aware of here are the bank of flowers and Fence 4. If you were to go round the bank of flowers you would probably have to go round Fence 4 as well in order to get a good line to Fence 9. This is a very long way round so it will probably be better to turn inside the bank of flowers, especially if the time is tight. Bear in mind though that much will depend on the distance between 9 and the following parallel: more white rails with a water tray underneath.

The distance between 9 and **10** walks 19 yards or 57 ft (7.4m), that is about 3¾ horse strides. As this is a soft four strides, turning inside the flowers should help you because you will probably not get a long stride to Fence 9. If the distance between 9 and 10 had been long you might

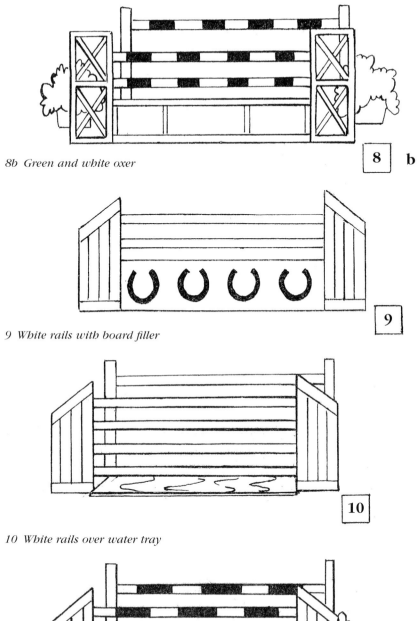

8b Green and white oxer

8 **b**

9 White rails with board filler

9

10 White rails over water tray

10

11 Orange and black parallel with walls

11

have needed to keep going round the flowers in order to get the right approach to 9.

The last fence, **11,** is an orange and black parallel with a good ground-line of walls. With its three poles and distinctive colours this is a solid looking fence. The distance from 10 to 11 walks 29 yards or 87 ft (25.6m), that is 6¼ horse strides. However, there is a slight dog-leg to 11 so both riders should aim to go on six strides. If time is tight this will help you to gain valuable seconds. When you jump No. 10 you should go in a direct line to 11, cutting out the curl in the turn. With a bold-looking fence you can do this: the horse should get a good round jump and have sufficient spring to make the back rail.

Be aware that the finish line is some little distance away, so you should ride forwards again on landing until you are across the line. There is nothing worse than jumping a clear round and picking up a time fault purely because you were too slow.

Having walked the course, before leaving the arena you should run quickly through it in your mind, like this:

Number 1

• Come on the right rein past the entrance, back on ourselves, slightly overshooting the turn to No. 2.

Number 2

• Aiming towards the judges' box, a little left-handed turn so we don't confuse the horse with No. 5 backwards.

Number 3 to Number 4

• As we land at No. 3, turn right-handed, to 4, 5 and 6 (four strides forward for Tom on both distances, for Sarah a soft, waiting jump over the stile, waiting five strides to the planks, waiting 5 strides to the oxer).

Number 6 to Number 7

• Look ahead to No. 7, the gate. Keep travelling to No.7 and pick up the rhythm to the combination.

Number 8

• A good solid jump in over 8a, waiting over 8b, waiting for the horse to shorten from 8b to 8c coming out.

Number 8 to Number 9
- Turn right-handed, inside the flowers. A nice soft jump over No. 9 because we know it's a soft four strides to No. 10, the water tray.

Number 9 to Number 10
- Waiting four strides to No. 10.

Number 10 to Number 11
- Direct line, no curl, on six strides to the last fence.
- Little squeeze, keep body up as the horse lands, keep cantering forward through the finish.

Riding the course
Now we are going to follow first Tom, then Sarah, as they jump the course and see the sorts of mistakes that they could so easily make. Quite a few horses have already finished with the odd time fault, so we know that they must go inside the flowers to Fence 9.

TOM'S ROUND
After making his salute, Tom has 45 seconds from when the bell goes to when he must cross the start beam. I have instructed him to show his horse the water tray because the sunlight has been bouncing off it and although the distance to it is a little short a lot of horses have been backing off. Tom is going to walk his horse past No. 10 as if he were going towards the combination – not blatantly showing him the fence but just letting him have a gentle look at it.

He sets off in a good solid canter and jumps Fence 1 nicely. However, the horse lands on the wrong leg so he has to make a flying change back on to the left lead. At No. 2 he is a little forward, too strong in his rhythm, which results in him getting a bit too close to 3. Although Tom tries to hold him off, the horse unfortunately leaves a leg and knocks Fence 3 down. He clears No. 4 without any problem and gets four nice strides to the planks and again to No. 6; but having landed over 6 he goes three strides before thinking where the next fence is. As a result he overshoots the line to 7 and comes at it slightly from left to right, which means that on landing he is aiming at the gap between 8 nd 10. He has to pull a little left-handed then right-handed to approach No. 8 and the horse is looking confused and going disunited. He has the first part of the combination down and is a long way off 8b. As a result he makes

*Tom and his
big-striding
Warmblood.*

up too much ground from 8b to 8c and has 8c down as well. All this happened because Tom did not look at that turn soon enough.

He makes a good turn inside the flowers, pops over 9, goes on four waiting strides to 10 and jumps that beautifully. He gets the six strides to No. 11 and jumps that perfectly too, finishing two seconds inside the time.

To sum up: Tom's problems were caused by being late in looking for the turn to the gate at 7 which meant that he overshot the turn and was not aiming towards the combination at 8. Trying to get straight for the combination resulted in the horse becoming disunited and having to go forward on an unbalanced stride. Fortunately, after that he got a grip and came home very well. Tom will have learnt something from that mistake.

SARAH'S ROUND

Sarah, who has a different agenda, has watched Tom's round and seen him make the four strides between Fences 4 and 5, and Fences 5 and 6 look easy. She asks if she should still go for five strides but just because she has seen someone else do it on four there is no reason to change her original plan. She should go for five, which will suit her horse better. She should also have a look at that water tray before starting her round.

As she sets off she is on the wrong leg, but there is no need to panic; there is time to change leg and get into a good canter. She makes a nice turn to No. 1, slightly overshooting it, and jumps 2 well. Her horse, who doesn't have the biggest stride in the world, puts in three normal strides to 3. She then makes an excellent turn round the bank of flowers to the stile. However, she is a bit forward here, changes her mind as she approaches 5 and goes for four strides. The horse has to put in a little stride at the end and hits the planks. She goes from 5 to 6 on five strides and jumps 6 perfectly. I think that she was swayed a little after all by Tom's performance there.

She gets a good turn to 7 but needs to be a little more forward going to 8. The horse puts in a super jump at 8a, clears 8b and is on a waiting stride coming out. But Sarah has missed cutting inside the bank of flowers and is having to go all the way round them which is a pity. She gets a nice distance to 9 and goes on four strides to 10. She is heading a little from left to right after 10 and has made an outside curl – which means that she makes seven strides to 11. She clears the last but unfortunately is one and a half seconds over the time allowed, so she picks up two time faults.

To sum up: if Sarah had gone inside the flowers to 9 she would have finished inside the time. Also, the extra stride to number 11 didn't help, certainly adding at least a second to the clock. But overall, with just that one little mistake at Fences 4 to 5, it was a good round.

*   *   *

The above examples show just how costly a slight lack of concentration, or a last-minute change of mind, can be. It's all a question of experience and confidence, and the more courses you jump the more you will learn how to be slightly ahead of yourself, which is something that I try to train people to do. When you're jumping a fence you should be thinking 'where should I be for the next one?'. It's rather like driving in heavy traffic: you think ahead and as a result you don't encounter any nasty surprises. Bear in mind, though, that the greater part of the rounds of each of our riders was good and that although they must be able to identify their mistakes they should not dwell on them. They must also be able to see what went right, and to promote those good points. If you become over-critical you will put too much pressure on your horse next time you compete.

The jump-off

If one or both of our riders had jumped clear they would have gone through to a jump-off over a course comprising Fences 1, 2, 5, 6, 7, 8a and 8b, 10 and 11. As you plan your route, remember that when jumping against the clock it is not just a question of being the fastest in a straight line. Fewer strides mean speed as well, so the fewer strides you take round the turns the faster you will be.

The jump-off course needs riding rather differently from the first round. You should begin by slightly overshooting the turn to No. 1 (on the left rein). Jump No. 1 slightly on the angle and aim towards the inside of No. 5, the planks. As you jump Fence 1 try to go as directly as you can to 2. You need to turn inside No. 9, so don't be too flat at 2. If you are a long way off 2 you will land a long way out and end up going round No. 9.

A soft jump over 2 will ensure that the horse lands flat-footed so that you can make the inside turn at 9 (the white vertical) on the way to the

Sarah and her three-quarter Thoroughbred.

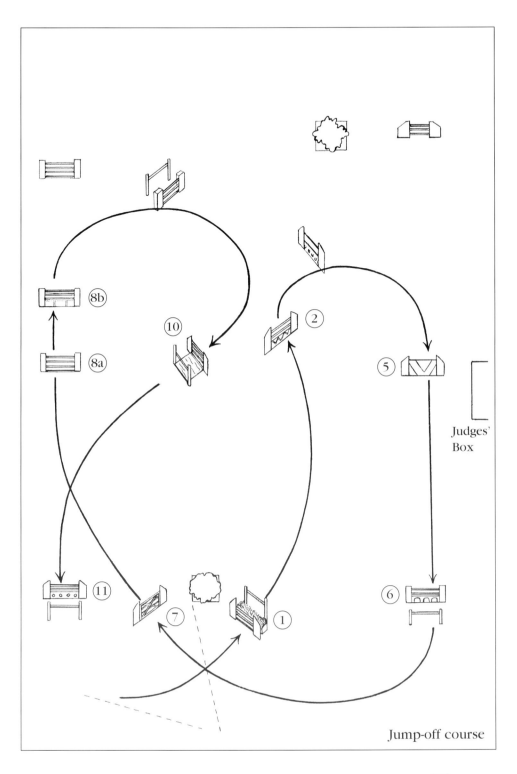

Judges'
Box

Jump-off course

planks at 5. Take four strides to No. 6 then make a neat turn to the gate at 7. Keep rolling down to the combination – there is plenty of room in the distance between 8a and 8b so you don't have to come in too 'backward'. Jump in, sit up a little for 8b and as you land over it turn right-handed inside No. 3 and No. 9 and so back to the water tray. You must be careful here to ensure that the horse doesn't think he is going to jump Fence 2. Take a little time to make sure that he knows where he is going. Where many riders will go wrong is in making the turn inside Fences 3 and 9 and allowing the horse to take them to Fence 2. They will then have to say 'No, not that one' and that's when everything can fall apart. As you jump out of the combination, make a good correct turn around your leg to No. 10, then straighten up the line and head for the last.

Riding the course in this way should take out all the surprise elements. When jumping against the clock, always remember that you can only go as fast as you can jump clear. You must try to leave the jumps up. You should be aware of your strengths and weaknesses, what your horse is good at and what he is less good at. For example, if he is inclined to spook at water trays, give him a bit of room turning to No. 10. By doing that you will be better off than making a very tight turn and having the horse stop. All too often you will hear a rider say, 'I knew he was going to do that.' Well, if they knew it, they should not have approached the fence in that way!

Remember that your horse won't win all the competitions that suit him – so he is even less likely to win those that don't suit him.

8

Top Tips

Day-to-day management

Devise a routine and programme for your horse. If you have a positive outlook the chances are that your horse will too.

Know your horse or pony's legs: any little lumps, bumps or windgalls which are normal for him. This will enable you to notice any changes straight away.

If your horse has a dry mouth, give him a sugar lump or mint just before your start working or jumping him: it will make him salivate.

Use a 50-50 mixture of methylated spirits and witch hazel for minor cuts and fly bites.

Use salt water for hardening skin around minor wounds.

For a sore mouth use a bit coated with sponge that has been soaked in a mixture of alum – dissolve one 5ml spoonful of powder in half a pint of warm water.

Use a mixture of vinegar and water as a fly repellant.

Use babies' disposable nappies when putting poultices on feet: they are soft and easy to secure on awkward horses.

In winter use a duvet under your horse's rug instead of a blanket. It will prevent his mane being rubbed out and will also be lighter on his back.

If you compete during the summer, keep your horse clipped: it will prevent him from sweating unduly and will save you time.

For summer clipping, use a fine blade to give a closer cut.

Turn-out
For a sharper appearance, trim your horse's ears, heels and head whiskers with small clippers.

Use a disposable razor to remove whiskers the day before a show.

Use Vaseline to brighten your horse's features.

Add some soda crystals or Dettol to hot water and use it to wipe the horse over after grooming: it will leave his coat clean and shiny.

Use pure alcohol on stable stains: it gets grey horses sparkling clean.

Use a fly-repellant gel to put the finishing touch to your horse's nose and round his eyes.

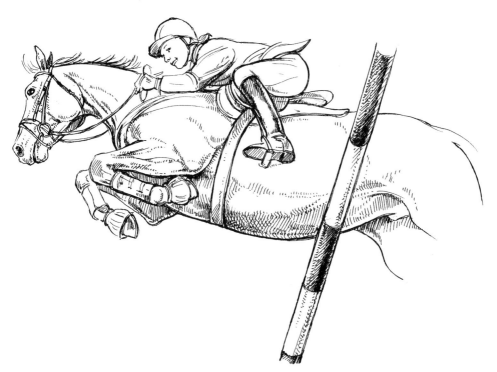

Tack matters

Make sure that your tack not only fits well but is also kept clean and in good repair. Remember that tack breaks mostly when you are using it, which can be very dangerous.

Melt down some glycerine saddle soap, add full-fat milk and a dash of leather dressing and leave in a 'fridge or cold area to set: it lasts longer than pure saddle soap and keeps tack supple and sparkling. (For three bars of saddle soap add half a pint of milk.)

Use Brasso wadding rather than liquid to clean brass buckles: it is less messy.

Wrap self-adhesive latex bandage around bits and curb chains to make them softer.

Use cheekpieces and reins that fasten with clips rather than buckles: they are quicker to release if you need to change a bit.

Use rubber or laced reins: plain leather becomes slippery when wet.

Always try to mount from a block rather than from the ground to avoid twisting and stretching your saddle. Older horses particularly find it harder to counterbalance the rider when you mount from the ground.

Use cheese-grater stirrup grips on your irons to help prevent your feet slipping out.

Use liquid boot polish on brushing boots to keep them clean and shiny.

Use an elastic band to tighten up loose keepers on bridles. It will also come in handy to prevent rosette ribbons flapping about should you win one!

Safety first

Always have someone on the ground with you when you are jumping. They don't have to be experts but they can put the jumps up for you and help in the event of an accident.

When mounted always wear a correctly fitting hat with the harness fastened.

When schooling, use flat planks on the ground rather than poles: they are safer should a horse step on them.

Use a stud guard when jumping, to prevent the horse injuring himself.

Stud care

After removing jumping studs, pick out the stud holes and pack them with cotton wool soaked in oil: this stops the holes filling up with dirt and makes it easier to screw the studs in next time.

For the best leverage, use a long-handled adjustable spanner for screwing in and removing studs.

Be prepared

If you wear a skullcap, stick a piece of Velcro to the front to prevent the silk cover blowing off in windy weather.

If you wear a back protector, choose one that is easy to remove (in case you need to go to the loo in a hurry!).

119

Always have a spare button for your riding jacket in your inside pocket. You can replace it very quickly, using a safety pin if necessary. If buttons are going to come off they invariably do so at a show.

Fit a rein-stop on your whip to prevent it slipping through your hand.

For a great shine use Parade boot polish on your riding boots and stud guards.

If you have a velvet-covered hat, steam clean it with a boiling kettle: this will bring up the pile and make it look new.

Before you go to a show remember to study the rules of the various classes you've entered for.

On the road

Load the lorry or trailer the day before a show. Remember to have the vehicle's oil and water checked and make sure that everything will start.

Give yourself plenty of time to get to shows: allow for traffic hold-ups.

Keep medical kits for horse and rider in the lorry for emergencies.

When travelling long distances leave as much space as possible between horses so that you can work around them as necessary, putting on rugs, attending to bandages, etc.

If you want to feed your horse on a long journey, use a travel mix comprising bran and nuts to which you need only add a little water.

At the show

When you arrive at the show have two buckets of water at the ready, one for washing off a sweaty horse, one for giving him a drink.

In very hot weather find a tree to stand under to prevent your horse getting sunstroke and offer him sips of water regularly so that he doesn't become dehydrated.

If your horse won't drink, offer him some carrots: they contain plenty of fluid.

Use a fly hat to prevent midges biting your horse's ears and causing him to shake his head. A fly hat will also cut out noise.

Fix your number to your square saddle cloth with safety pins or tacking thread. It looks much smarter than tying it round your waist, and you are less likely to lose it.

Fasten your Pony Club tie to your shirt with a safety pin to prevent it coming loose and flapping about.

In wet going, wear a pair of rubber galoshes over your riding boots: they will keep the bottom of your boots clean for a better grip.

Put saddle soap on the insides of your riding boots just before you mount to give you extra grip when jumping.

Smear a little Vaseline around the inside of overreach boots to help them slip on more easily.

If your horse jumps in bandages, secure them with tape to prevent them from coming undone.

Use wet wipes to give your bridle a last-minute shine before you go into the arena.

In wet weather wear a pair of gloves (not leather) to help you grip the reins.

Always be polite to people at shows. Remember that a lot of them are voluntary workers: without them shows could not survive.

If you are not sure of anything, don't be afraid to ask a more experienced person for advice or help. Most people are only too pleased to oblige.

Try not to do too many competitions on one day. It is
better to have a fresh
horse or pony who is
trying to please
rather one who is
tired and wanting
to go home.

Preparing to jump

Be at the collecting
ring half an hour
before you are due
to jump so that your
horse can get used to
the atmosphere.

Have a ring-bag prepared to carry
your whip, spurs, hat, towel, hole
punch, length of string, safety pins, tape and a drink.

If possible, have a few friends at the collecting ring to help hold your
horse while you walk the course or look at the jump-off.

Have a towel handy at the ring to clean your boots just before you
mount and for wiping sweaty reins or slobber from your horse's
mouth.

For safety, when warming up in the collecting ring always call out the
jump which you are going to – 'Vertical, please' or 'Oxer, please' – so
that other rides know where you are heading.

Have your horse ready to go – girths tightened, stirrups down – 15
horses before you are due to jump.

Watch other riders' rounds to see where the problems are on the
course.

In very wet conditions try to go at the start of the competition – that way you will get the best of the ground. Far too many riders think 'It's raining, I'll go at the end.' That is a mistake: the wetter the ground the worse the going.

When you enter the ring make a quick check to see that all the poles, etc, are sitting correctly in their cups. Pay particular attention to gates and planks, as these are on flat cups and they could be right on the edge.

After your round
Always reward your pony when he has finished his round, with a mint or other favourite treat. He will have tried his best.

Remove your horse's tendon boots and loosen his girth and noseband when you have finished jumping: it will speed up his recovery time

Wash mud off your horse immediately: it is much harder to remove when dry.

Analyse your round afterwards to identify what went wrong and decide what could be improved. Try to identify the good parts as well: this will help you to know your own strengths as well as your weaknesses.

If a particularly spooky fence has caused you major problems, ask the show organiser if you could train over it when the show has ended. If this is not possible, try to recreate the fence at home and practise over it.

The jump-off
Check the jump-off course and if necessary practise any turns before you go into the arena.

Always try to watch the first rider go in a jump-off and make a note of his time. When your turn comes you will be able to judge where you need to save time.

AND FINALLY...

Choose short names for your horses and ponies: they won't give you
writer's cramp when you're filling in entry forms - and they are
cheaper to have engraved on trophies!

Index